Extraordinary Parsons

of

Devon and Cornwall

Emily Clay

DEVON BOOKS

First published in Great Britain in 1986 by Devon Books

ISBN: 0 86114–780–4

British Library Cataloguing-in-Publication Data
Clay, Emily
Extraordinary parsons of Devon and Cornwall.
1. Church of England–England–Cornwall–Clergy–Biography
2. Church of England–England–Devon–Clergy–Biography
I. Title
283'.092'2   BX5197

Printed and bound in Great Britain by A. Wheaton & Co. Ltd

DEVON BOOKS
Official Publisher to Devon County Council
Devon Books is a division of A. Wheaton & Co. Ltd, which represents:

Editorial, Design, Publicity, Production and Manufacturing
A. Wheaton & Co. Ltd
Hennock Road, Marsh Barton, Exeter, Devon EX2 8RP
Tel: 0392 74121; Telex 42749 (WHEATN G)
(A. Wheaton & Co. Ltd is a member of the
Pergamon/B.P.C.C. Group of Companies)

Sales and Distribution
Town & Country Books, P.O. Box 31, Newton Abbot, Devon TQ12 5AQ
Tel: 08047 2690

Extraordinary Parsons

of

Devon and Cornwall

For my parents and my sister Janet

Contents

Acknowledgements

I would like to thank the staff of Brixham Public Library and the staff of the reference department of Torquay Public Library for their kindness and efficient help. I also wish to thank Mrs B. K. Smith and Mrs K. M. Johnson for help in so many ways on visits to numerous churches.

The photographs on pp. 3, 29, 30, 35, 40, 42, 47 and 58 are reproduced by courtesy of the Westcountry Studies Library, Exeter; the remaining photographs are by the author.

CHAPTER ONE

The Parson's Lot

THIS BOOK IS not intended to poke fun at the clergymen of Devon and Cornwall or to belittle their good work. They are, as we tend to forget, human and have the same idiosyncrasies and human qualities found in us all but because they are in the public eye, their eccentricities or misdemeanours are often magnified.

Before the days of state aid for the sick and poor, the parson, and sometimes the squire, were the only people the poor could turn to for help. The parson, often out of his meagre pay or private means, provided food, clothing and fuel for the destitute. He also acted as doctor, letter writer and reader to his parishioners, many of whom were illiterate. He taught in the school, of which he often helped to finance the building, equipping and running. All this was besides his usual theological work. Many of the parishes were large and the dwellings widely scattered, which made the parson's work more difficult. Lydford parish, which covers the whole of Dartmoor, is said to be the largest in England.

Often the parson was in need of help himself. His living conditions were frequently very bad, though the parson of St Ives must have been exaggerating his hardship when he complained to Francis Kilvert, the diarist parson, of the appalling stench of fish which he had to endure: sometimes it was so bad, he said, that it stopped the church clock.

Some of the vicarages were very large, even for the size of family prevalent in the nineteenth century and earlier, and were expensive to maintain. They were often very damp and cold. The Kingsleys had constant trouble with a damp vicarage and the Revd W. Davy's death is said to have been due to his catching cold when moving into the damp parsonage.

In many villages the vicarage was the only house with sizeable rooms, so it was used for various parish functions, such as meetings and Bible classes, and the church fête was held in the garden, so the parson's home must sometimes have seemed to be the home of his villagers too. But these vicarages would have seemed like palaces to the poor curate of Shute who could find no accommodation other than his church, which must have been uncomfortable to sleep in as the chancel had no roof and

1

the doors did not fasten. The unfortunate incumbent of Lydford whose parsonage was a poor cottage had to sleep under his umbrella when it rained heavily.

At the other end of the scale were the parsons who lived in manor houses. The vicarage at Bude Haven was Elford Manor and the original rectory at Little Hempston was also a manor house. The Revd H.A. Simcoe of Penheale near Launceston lived in an old mansion. The vicar of Great Torrington had a moated manor house presented to him in 1491 by Margaret Beaufort, Countess of Richmond, because she felt sorry for him having to walk so far from the church to his home. Margaret's son, Henry VII, had given it to her. Cardinal Wolsey held the living from 1510 to 1511 but probably never visited the house. No doubt the vicar of Dartmouth, the Revd Nicholas Battersby, would have welcomed such a benefactor for when the council needed a new guildhall they requisitioned his house, now a hardware shop, overruling the poor man's objections.

Parsons' stipends varied considerably throughout Devon and Cornwall according to the value of the living. Many of the nineteenth-century parsons had private means and several came from aristocratic families. The thirteenth Earl of Devon is included in the list of vicars of Powderham church. The youngest son of the family was often expected to enter the church. As the advowson of the local church probably belonged to his father, a living was guaranteed for him. Sometimes the parson was the squire himself (such as Baring-Gould), for whom the term 'squarson' has been coined. The parson was responsible for paying his curate. Many curates were very poorly paid; where the living was a rich one, this was the result of greed on the parson's part, but many parsons, who were forced to employ curates because of overwork, old age or illness, must have endured poverty to do so.

When Bishop Phillpotts was endeavouring to improve the pay of curates, he said that he hoped none received less than £40 and few below £50 a year. The plight of some curates is emphasized by an entry in Crockford's Clerical Dictionary of 1903. It concerned the Revd F. J. Bleasby who had been unemployed for three years despite twenty-three years' experience as a curate and 470 applications for curacies. As he had been unable to obtain a post, he had been forced to enter Tiverton workhouse. The Revd Francis Lyte wrote that after deductions from his stipend for a curate and for a house, if one were built for him, all he would have would be the house and £25 a year. The house was never built. He was lucky he had a private income.

The collection of tithes sometimes caused difficulties. St Enodoc church which is close to the shore was engulfed by sand and at one period the parson and his clerk had to climb into the church through a hole in the roof to hold an annual service so that the right to the tithes might continue.

In order to supplement the meagre living of a poor parish a vicar might take another living. Sometimes some of the clergy who were well off held several livings from sheer greed. Thomas Brerewode was one of the worst

Sabine Baring-Gould, rector of Lewtrenchard

3

offenders. According to Goodenough, he was vicar of Colyton and had three other livings, was an archdeacon and a vicar general, a chancellor of Exeter Cathedral and held an Oxford fellowship.

Professor Hoskins in *Devon* tells us that nearly half the livings were held in plurality in Devon. Subsidiary livings were either served by a curate or the parson went from one parish to the other to take the services, which meant that the number of services in each was curtailed. The parson who held the livings of Eggesford and Mariansleigh is an example: he held one service in each parish in summer but none in winter, giving the excuse of short days and bad roads.

One of the results of plurality of livings was that the parson did not live in the parish although this could also stem from such causes as lack of a suitable house in the parish, illness or leave of absence for study. Bishop Phillpotts of Exeter was particularly anxious to remedy non-residence in his diocese, which at that time included both Devon and Cornwall. According to a visitation questionnaire for 1883 there were 384 non-resident incumbents. Three had no churches and the rest were mainly non-resident because of housing difficulties.

Certainly there had been cases which needed attention, such as that of the vicar of Bigbury who had been in Spain for five years and the vicar of Hartland who was thought to be in London although this was not certain. Surely one of the oddest excuses given for non-residence must have been that of Parson Elford of North Petherwin who, when his bishop remonstrated with him, said that he could not possibly live in a place where there was no barber to curl his wig.

If the non-residency of some clergy indicates a certain lack of concern for the parish, there were others who were deeply concerned for their parishioners' wellbeing. One such was the Revd Edward Girdleston of Halberton.

The lot of the peasantry in Devon and Cornwall in the nineteenth century was certainly grim. Wages of farm labourers were very low, sometimes only 7s. a week with no perks other than some very rough cider. Housing was very poor. The work was hard and the hours long, often for the labourer's wife too, whose work might be part of the contract. A labourer's active life could be over at fifty or earlier when he was dependent on the rates for existence.

The conditions shocked the Revd, later Canon, Edward Girdleston who had come from Lancashire where wages were much higher. He tried to obtain better wages and conditions for the labourers by discussing the matter with the farmer employers, but got no satisfaction from them. When the cattle plague was rampant, he preached a pointed sermon, 'Behold the hand of the Lord is upon thy cattle', suggesting that is was a judgement on them. The farmers were furious and went to chapel instead of church, but the chapel preacher, a friend of Girdleston, told them to go back. Despite the farmers' persecution Girdleston was determined to help the peasants and with the aid of funds from sympathizers throughout the country, he helped many of them to migrate to other districts where conditions were better. They in turn as they prospered helped members of their families and friends to join them so that by the time Girdleston himself had left, between 400 and 500 of the labourers had settled in other parts of the country. Labour around Halberton was becoming scarce and the farmers were forced to pay considerably higher wages. Joseph Arch, who continued Girdleston's work, formed the first farm labourers' trade union.

Despite the poverty and suffering with which the parsons came into contact, their lives were not devoid of humour. Sydney Smith, the witty and popular parson, proved this. He has left an amusing description of Tug, Lug, Haul and Crawl, the four oxen he acquired on the advice of a neighbouring gentleman to haul building material for the house he was building; 'but Tug and Lug took to fainting and required buckets of sal-volatile, and Haul and Crawl to lie down in the mud. So I did as I ought to have done at first, took the advice of the farmer instead of the gentleman; sold my oxen, bought a team of horses.'

It raises a chuckle too to read of Jack Russell going hunting in his nightshirt when a fox was taking his wife's turkeys. He slipped a coat over his nightshirt, saddled his horse, let out his hounds and hunted the killer by moonlight. When he returned to bed some time later, he presented his wife with the brush, telling her that her turkeys were safe.

Although it was not funny at the time, no doubt the vicar of St Breward and his wife could laugh afterwards. They had been to Bodmin on a shopping expedition and were late leaving the town. Before they could get home they were caught in such a thick fog that they could not see where they were going and soon were completely lost. They therefore decided to stay where they were until morning and wrapped themselves in rugs for a long wait. The pony was very restless so the vicar unharnessed him. When daylight came and the fog lifted, they found themselves at the gate of their own vicarage which the pony had recognized.

Names can cause amusement. An eighteenth-century parson of Moretonhampstead was appropriately called the Revd Micaiah Toogood. A 'squarson' on Lundy Island had the surname of Heaven; the island was jocularly referred to as 'The Kingdom of Heaven' since his ancestor had bought Lundy in 1836.

According to Baring-Gould, the vicar of Helland had gone to town and asked a friend to arrange for the Archdeacon of Cornwall to take his Sunday service for him so that he need not come back for it. The telegram in reply read, 'The Archdeacon of Cornwall is going to Hell and you need not return.'

Several amusing tales are told of Devon and Cornish vicars. Goodenough told the story of parson Parramore of Dunterton who was interrupted during a service by a querulous parishioner who informed him that he was paid to speak up and that they could not hear him at the back of the church. Parramore then shouted that the objector owed him two years' rent and wanted to know whether he could hear that. Then there was the Pinhoe vicar who when his donkey died dug a grave for it which was too shallow; the parson was either too lazy or too exhausted by his efforts to dig it any deeper so the donkey's ears remained sticking above ground. It is said, no doubt with tongue in cheek, that the vicar of Bampton, the Revd Bartholomew Davey could attribute his Cambridge qualifications to an amusing whim of his heiress wife. She did not like the colour of his Oxford gown so sent him to Cambridge instead.

St Leger Gordon has written of the vicar of Hennock who is reputed to have trapped a thief by an astute trick. Someone had stolen a goose from one of the villagers. The parson made it known that he would expose the thief during the next service. He preached to a large congregation on the sin of theft and mentioned the loss of the goose. Then he said that he knew who had taken it because as he looked at the thief he could see an incriminating feather on his nose. The thief surreptitiously felt at his nose and was denounced by the vicar. The story was also told by the Revd H. Miles Brown but was attributed to the Revd William Score, vicar of Whitestone 1736-87, who exposed a potato thief by the same ruse.

Although the rather mean trick played on the parson of Tiverton may seem amusing to some, it could not have been funny for the poor parson. He complained to the Earl of Devon, his patron, of the excessive size of his parish and of his low stipend. The Earl promised to do something about it, which he did by reducing both the parish and the income to a quarter of their former value.

Ottery St Mary church

6

Parsons using others' sermons, though often ridiculed, sometimes caused amusement. Jack Russell was ordered to preach at one of Bishop Phillpotts' visitations. The Bishop was fulsome in his praise of the sermon. Russell said he agreed as he always thought it one of Barrow's best. (Isaac Barrow was a seventeenth-century theologian.) A similar story is told of a curate of Ottery St Mary who was preaching his first sermon. His vicar, Dr Cornish, condescendingly said that it was not bad for a first sermon. The curate said that credit was due not to him but to Bishop Andrews as it was one of his best sermons.

Margaret A. Courtney tells the story of a vicar of Cubert who was asked to say grace at a house where he was given rabbit. At several other places earlier he had also been served with rabbit, which he hated. His grace was:

> Of rabbits young and rabbits old,
> Of rabbits hot and rabbits cold,
> Of rabbits tender, rabbits tough,
> I thank the Lord we've had enough.

Today most clergy have a comparatively short stay in their parishes. As the majority do not have a private fortune they move on to ensure a reasonable standard of living. In the nineteenth century, however, despite the number of poor livings in Devon and Cornwall, the clergy, many of whom had private means, stayed to serve their parishes for long periods. A number served for over fifty years: Peter Dyke Ackland of Broadclyst and Henry Manning of Stokeinteignhead both served for fifty-one years, Henry Oxland was rector of Illogan for fifty-three years, a rector of Lustleigh was there for fifty-six years and there are several other examples.

Those serving for sixty years or more are not so numerous, but among them may be cited: Thomas Boyce of Drendon and Samuel Belfield of Paignton (sixty-one years); three clergy of Buckland Monachorum, Joseph Rowe (sixty-two years), Charles Barter (sixty-three years) and Richard Hayne (sixty-five years); William Palk of Ashcombe (sixty-five years). Robert Hole, who was rector of North Tawton, served his parish for sixty-six years and so did Thomas Pyle of Malborough and Thomas Potbury of Payhembury. An outstandingly long service is that of the Revd Charles Baxter who was vicar of Cornworthy for seventy-one years, but an even longer one can be claimed by the Revd Wrothersley Wingfield who was vicar of Gulval for seventy-three years.

Robert Hole, mentioned above, was the last of a succession of rectors of that family (with a break of only five years) who served the parish for 200 years. At Offwell in East Devon the Copplestone family have served the church continuously from 1770 to the twentieth century. The Carwithens of Manaton have produced nine of its rectors and at Phillack rectors of the Hockin family have been preaching in the church for three centuries.

Many Devonshire and Cornish parsons are long lived. Robert Hole was ninety-two, Richard Reynolds of Stoke Fleming, who was hounded from his parish during the Civil War, was in his hundredth year when he died.

7

The Revd Harry Clement Williams of Paignton, who was 102 when he died in 1981, was the oldest clergyman in Britain. In 1982 the Revd Sydney Stevens died at the age of ninety-four: he was thought to be the oldest working clergyman in the Church of England.

E.V. Thompson, in *Discovering Cornwall's South Coast*, mentions an even older gentleman, the rector of Landewednack who was said to be 120 years old when he walked 26 miles from Landewednack to Penryn.

A surprising number of parishes can list their clergy as far back as the thirteenth century. The first rector of Kilkhampton, Geoffry Fitztheodore, was rector until 1202. Some other parishes with such lists are Shebbear (1204), Hennock (1207), Brixham (1228), Cheriton Fitzpaine (1256), Powderham (1258) and St Gerran's (1260). Some lists, such as those at Ugborough and Cheriton Fitzpaine, link the incumbencies with historical events, which adds considerably to their interest.

CHAPTER TWO

History

SEVERAL PARSONS HAVE played a notable part, sometimes unwillingly, in the history of the two counties and of the country.

In A.D. 1001, in the time of Ethelred the Unready, there was a fierce battle between the Saxons and the invading Danes at Pinhoe. During the fighting the Saxons' supply of arrows became dangerously low. A brave and resourceful Saxon priest managed to get through the enemy lines to Exeter and to return with a fresh supply of arrows, but unfortunately this did not ensure a victory for the Saxons. Many were killed and the Danes burnt the village of Pinhoe. A small sum of money was awarded to the valiant priest; although, as Creswell pointed out, this was probably not in recognition of his valour but to pay for masses for the dead. The grant continued to be paid until the present century and may still be in existence; it is the oldest grant paid by the Ecclesiastical Commissioners.

Aldred, a priest at Denbury near Newton Abbot, became the first Saxon bishop and crowned both Harold and William the Conqueror. There was an unfortunate misunderstanding at the latter's coronation: when Aldred asked the crowd if they consented to the crowning, the roar of assent was so great that the guards outside the abbey thought that William was being murdered and threw lighted torches on the roofs of the surrounding buildings. Although Aldred has been much derided, he gave generously to religious institutions including those of Beverley, Gloucester, Southwell and Worcester. He gave the manor of Denbury to Tavistock Abbey, of which he was abbot in 1027.

Bishop Walter Stapledon was born probably in 1261 in North Devon. He was the younger son of Sir Richard Stapledon and, like many of the younger sons of aristocratic families, entered the Church. He became rector of Aveton Gifford and later Bishop of Exeter. At his enthronement the street was covered in black cloth which was later cut up and given to the poor. He founded the Guild of St Lawrence at Ashburton and gave it a chapel, paying £4.13s. a year for prayers to be said for his soul after his death. He also founded the Oxford college later known as Exeter College.

Eventually he became Treasurer of the Realm of England under Edward

II. The king could not have been an easy man to work for, but Stapledon was a learned and capable man and no doubt a diplomatic one too.

When Isabella landed from France, Edward vacated London for the safety of Lundy Island and left Stapledon to cope with the emergency. Stapledon promptly excommunicated Isabella and her forces. Rebellion ensued and the mob caught and killed him in 1326 as he was returning to his inn to dinner and he was unable to reach the sanctuary of St Paul's. The queen later granted him a Christian burial and he is reputed to be buried in Exeter cathedral.

Wolsey was a non-resident rector of Great Torrington for a short time. One of his successors to the living during the Civil War must have had a shock when his church was blown up. It had been used as a royalist arsenal and was later employed as a prison by the victorious General Fairfax. In the darkness the gunpowder somehow became ignited and the church was blown up. Two hundred men were killed and Fairfax nearly lost his life too.

When we hear that Francis Babington, a chaplain of the Earl of Leicester, preached at the funeral of Amy Robsart, it conjures up all the mystery of her tragic death at Cumnor in Oxfordshire and all the intrigue of the Elizabethan court. Babington's ministry at Holsworthy was very short (seven months): as he was out of favour with Leicester and, worse still, suspected of being a papist, he thought it diplomatic to flee the country.

The clergy were very much involved in the ill-fated Prayer-book Rebellion. The 1549 Act of Uniformity which stipulated that the new

The church house, Sampford Courtenay

10

prayer-book had to be used was very unpopular. The congregation of Sampford Courtenay particularly resented it and forced the priest, William Harper, to use the old prayer-book, despite admonishments from local Justices of Peace. Matters came to a head when William Hellyons, who had rebuked the villagers, was killed as he came down the church house stairs. The rebels gathered others from Devon and Cornwall and marched on Exeter which they besieged. However, Lord Russell, sent to quell the revolt with an army of German and Italian mercenaries, routed them at Fenny Bridges and lifted the siege of Exeter. He put down the rising with much cruelty, being particularly ruthless in his treatment of the rebel priests. One tragic case was that of Robert Walsh who was born at Penryn, and was at the time of the rebellion vicar of St Thomas church, Exeter. Despite his calling, he was skilled in the use of weapons (crossbow and gun) and took an active part in the rising. When he was captured he was condemned without trial and hanged from his own church tower dressed in his mass vestments. It was a particularly hard fate as it was he who had saved Exeter by dissuading the rebels from burning it to the ground. The vicar of Poundstock and the vicar of St Veep were also hanged for their part in the same rebellion.

Daniel Defoe tells us in *A Tour through England and Wales* that the Revd John Moreman was famous for being the first clergyman in England to teach the Lord's Prayer, the Creed and the Commandments in English and to read them to the congregation of his church of Menheniot.

Robert Herrick, John Weeks and James Forbes, who became rector of Bovey Tracey, all took part as chaplains in the expedition to the island of Rhé to aid La Rochelle. Buckingham was in command of the expedition. He beseiged St Martins, the main fort on the island, but failed to take it. Preparations for the expedition were inadequate: for instance, there were supplies of wheat but no grinding or cooking facilities. Food supplies were low, shelter was lacking and illness was rife. The retreat was badly organized: some of the men were killed and the colours were lost, and on the return voyage some of the ships were wrecked.

Herrick was one of the parsons displaced by Cromwell after the Civil War. Perhaps he did not mind so much as some, as not only did he love London and dislike Devonshire, or so he said, but he had friends, relations and patrons in London who no doubt looked after him until he was reinstated, which happened in 1662.

In theory the deposed parsons could be granted one fifth of the value of the living, but few gained this benefit as the conditons attached were so stringent and the slightest thing could invalidate the claim.

A few were lucky in the intruding ministers who came to replace them. Samuel Tapper who moved into the vicarage at Tiverton allowed the deposed vicar half of the proceeds of the living and a house in the glebe. The puritan intruding rector at St Just-in-Roseland was so popular with his congregation that at the Restoration he was given special permission to stay in the parish and he and the royalist parson who replaced him became

11

great friends. Another amicable arrangement occurred at St Mellion where the returning royalist vicar, Mr Granger, allowed the parson he was replacing to rent his glebe farm and to share his vicarage. The intruding parsons were lowly people, many of them servants and tradesmen. The parson at Sampford Peverell must have been pleased when he returned to find that the intruding parson, who had once been a ship's carpenter, had left a table he had made.

Some parsons suffered greatly after the Civil War, not only through poverty but also from persecution and cruelty. The Revd Henry Smith of Cornwood, a royalist, was persecuted for his allegiance to King Charles, he was imprisoned and died in gaol. Sheer bravery saved Peter Grigg, a Brixham curate, from dying for his faith. He was saying the Lord's Prayer during a service at Churston church when a soldier ordered him to stop and put his pistol to Grigg's head. The curate ignored him and finished the prayer, then said that he had done his duty as a priest and the man had better do his as a soldier. The man slunk away ashamed.

Richard Reynolds was hounded out of his parish of Stoke Fleming near Dartmouth. His goods were stolen and he escaped imprisonment by dressing up as a farmer. He met the soldiers looking for him and actually directed them. Then he rode as fast as he could into Cornwall where he was forced to hide in the mines. His wife finally secured his safety by payment of a hundred pounds. When he returned the soldiers were billeted on him, but he became friendly with them. Later he had to leave the parish and go to Woodleigh, his other parish, where his daughters made provision for him and his wife. He was reinstated at Stoke Fleming when Charles II came to the throne and when he died he was in his hundredth year.

The vicar of Molland, Daniel Berry, a staunch royalist, suffered greatly for his loyalty. Not only did he lose his living but everything he had was taken away from him, even his own bed. The Dean of Exeter, Dr William Peterson, and his wife were rather more fortunate in that though they lost their belongings, their beds were not taken. Peterson was deprived of his appointments and after his wife's death he went to London. There Cromwell saw him looking poverty-stricken and remarked to his companion that no doubt that man would be willing to die for his religion. The same day Peterson was tracked down to his home by a stranger who invited him to dine and afterwards left some money on the table for Peterson. Several times subsequently a gift of money was left which was thought to be from Cromwell. At the Restoration the office of Dean of Exeter was given back to Peterson.

William Lane, rector of Ringmore and incumbent of Aveton Gifford, took an active part in the Civil War. He drilled his parishioners to fight for the king and led them in the defence of Loddiswell Bridge. He ranged his battery of cannons on the hillside of Pittons, and when Cromwell's men tried to cross the river he fired at them until the guns could be used no longer. Then he spiked the guns and pushed them down the hillside before beating a hasty retreat for Ringmore where he hid in a room in the church tower for three months. The room can still be seen and is unusual in that it has a fireplace, although it is unlikely that Lane would have dared to use it. His parishioners fed him and he stayed there while an unsuspecting intruding minister was preaching in the church below. Cromwell's men were besieging Salcombe castle at the time and the rector's belligerence was causing difficulty in getting supplies to the soldiers. Men were therefore sent from Plymouth with orders to shoot him, but although they searched the rectory and the parish they could not find him. Lane intended to walk to London in search of a pardon and to walk back to his home in Devon; however, he died in Exeter and was buried in Alphington in 1654.

John Snell, rector of Thurlestone, went as chaplain to the besieged castle at Salcombe. When at last the royalists surrendered, they were allowed to leave to the beat of their drums with colours flying. One of the conditions granted at the surrender had been that Parson Snell should be permitted to return to his rectory. But he was not left in peace and his cattle and other effects were stolen and he himself had to flee for his life. His living was returned at the Restoration and he was also made a canon of the Cathedral Church of St Peter, Exeter, in recognition of his loyalty.

The parson of Buckland Filleigh was with the famous Cornish royalist Sir Bevil Grenville when he was killed leading the charge at Stamford Hill near Bath. He must have seen Anthony Payne, Grenville's giant servant, put the young son of Sir Bevil on his father's charger and shout to the dispirited men that a Grenville was still leading them so they should follow him.

Some of Cromwell's intruding ministers were not much better off than the parsons they had replaced. John Serle, the intruding parson who took over the parish of St Mary's Plympton, was £200 poorer when he left the parish than when he arrived, as the vicarage was in such a ruinous state that repairs cost more than his income for the two years.

These intruding parsons had as difficult a time after the Restoration as royalist ones had experienced during the Commonwealth. John Flavel of Dartmouth and his father, also a clergyman in London, were deprived of their livings. The father and his wife were imprisoned and died of plague, probably caught in prison. John Flavel continued to hold clandestine services in isolated places. One such place was reputed to be a rock exposed only at low water in the middle of Kingsbridge estuary. Flavel had several narrow escapes from capture. Later he had to flee to London where he wrote several books. When James II granted an indulgence Flavel returned to Dartmouth where his followers built a meeting-house for him.

The Revd William Yeo was the parson of Wolborough. He was a very zealous parson but refused to acknowledge the Church of England laws and was consequently deprived of his living. However, he continued to preach in secret, holding meetings in a pit (Puritans' Pit) in Bradley Woods. Attempts were made to arrest him but he evaded capture and after the Toleration Act became law he preached in a chapel in Wolborough until his death in 1699.

One of the founders of Massachusetts was a Devon parson, John Mavarick, vicar of Awliscombe and Beaworthy. An Oxford graduate, he was ordained deacon and priest on the same day. He died in Dorchester, Massachusetts in 1656.

> And shall Trelawny die?
> Then twenty thousand Cornish men will know the reason why.

Everyone knows those lines, but how many know much more about Trelawny or why his life was in danger? Sir Jonathan Trelawny is usually thought to be the subject of the song. However, Sir John Trelawny is also a likely contender.

Sir Jonathan Trelawny was born in 1650. His father was the second baronet and his mother was a Seymore of Berry Pomeroy. There seems to have been a history of prison sentences in the family. His grandfather was imprisoned in the Tower of London by order of the House of Commons before he was created a baronet and it has been suggested that the verse might refer to him. Sir Jonathan's father was imprisoned for his loyalty to Charles I.

After attending Westminster School and Christ Church, Oxford, where he obtained his B.A. and M.A. degrees, he was ordained and appointed to St Ives and Southill by his parents who had the advowson of the living. He became a baronet on the death of his brother. He married a Devon heiress, Rebecca Hele of Bascombe and there were six sons and six daughters of the marriage. One son became Governor of Jamaica, another was drowned with Sir Clowdisley Shovell when his ship was wrecked off the Scilly Isles and two became clergymen.

James sent Trelawny down to Cornwall when he expected the Duke of Monmouth to land there. Monmouth had already landed (in Dorset) when Trelawny reached Cornwall, but he signed the commissions and sent Rushleigh, the only deputy lieutenant willing to call out the militia, to inspect and place each regiment at a strategic position. Although Trelawny wanted the bishopric of Exeter he received that of Bristol for his services.

Although Trelawny was a staunch royalist, he did not approve of the king's aggressive papistry and the 1687 Declaration of Indulgence turned him against the king. He refused to sign it and, as a result of his influence, his clergy would not sign it either. He declared himself firmly of the Church of England and helped the French refugee Protestants in Bristol. When the second Declaration of Indulgence was produced he assisted in drawing up the bishops' petition against it. The result was that he, Sancroft, Archbishop of Canterbury, and five bishops were imprisoned in the Tower of London. They were released after a week and sent for trial but a verdict of not guilty was passed. The king removed Trelawny's name from the burgess roll of Liskeard.

Trelawny denied the rumour that he was involved in the invitation to

William of Orange to invade Britain. James tried to curry his favour by offering him the see of Exeter but Trelawny welcomed William's troops in Bristol and wrote a letter of welcome to William. After the coronation Trelawny obtained the coveted see of Exeter. He took measures to defend the town against the expected invasion of the French.

His sympathy with the later opposition of the Churchills and Princess Anne to the king, meant that he stayed away from the court for ten years, spending much time in his diocese and at his estate at Trelawne. When Anne came to the throne, he preached before her at St Paul's and was later promoted to the see of Winchester where he had a huge bishop's throne built. He died in 1721 and was buried in Pelynt church.

It is said that at that period clergy showed their allegiance by the types of trees they planted in their churchyards. Those favouring William of Orange planted limes and the Jacobites planted firs. Both North Tawton and Lewtrenchard have avenues of limes, but the species may have no political significance.

George Ireland officiated at three coronations — those of George IV, William IV and Victoria. The night before the coronation of George IV he stored all the regalia in his bedroom with a guard; it must have been a relief when he was able to hand it over the next morning. Son of an Ashburton butcher, he was for a time curate at Kingsteignton and travelled the continent as tutor to Lady Orford's son George Walpole, later Lord Clinton. Ireland became prebendary of Westminster, founded the scholarships named after him and a chair of theology at Oxford. On his death in 1842 he was buried in Westminster Abbey.

The Revd W. Jackman of Feock is believed to have been the last clergyman to take a service in Cornish, which he did until 1640. The last sermon in Cornish was said to have been preached at Landewednack in 1678.

Fitzroy Henry Richard Stanhope served in the Peninsular Wars and lost a leg in the battle of Waterloo. He was deprived of a pension because the pension list was full. The Prince Regent therefore gave him the living of St Buryan although he was not in orders. He was, however, soon ordained by the Bishop of Cork. The living, together with those of Sennen and St Leven, brought him a substantial income, although he left the parishes entirely in the hands of curates.

In 1784 the vicar of Tintagel had the curious experience of being the only man on the local electoral roll which meant that he sent two members to parliament.

CHAPTER THREE

Churches

MANY PARSONS GAVE generously to their churches. Baring-Gould, who did so much to restore his church at Lewtrenchard, gave a beautiful fifteenth-century chandelier, one of a pair which he bought from the Belgian church of Malines when they were replaced by gas lighting. Unfortunately the one at Lewtrenchard has been stolen, but the other, which he presented to Staverton where the family once owned property, still hangs in the church there. He also gave to Lewtrenchard church the painting over the altar and another of the crucifixion. He acquired the eagle lectern for his church when it was discarded from one in Brittany.

The beautiful carved chancel screen in Bridford church was given by an early-sixteenth-century rector, the Revd Walter Southcote. An interesting feature of the screen is the carving of the little figures in the panels in place of the more usual paintings. A more recent gift of a rood screen was from the Revd W. Wykes-Finch who gave the northern section of the one at South Tawton when it was installed in 1902.

One parson used most original tactics to improve the approach to his church. A Tavistock curate responsible for conducting the services at Brent Tor church found the scramble to the top of the tor exhausting, so he decided to build a pathway to the church which would make the journey much easier. However, he had difficulty in getting anyone to undertake the job. He therefore bought several bottles of whisky and when he found a man who looked strong he invited him to his home for a drink and plied him with whisky until the man was happy enough to give a day's work to the church. The path they built is no longer there but Baring-Gould, who gave us the account of its construction, adds ruefully that it badly damaged the inner wall of an ancient fortress.

Several parsons have retrieved church possessions or saved them from destruction. Samuel Rowe, a rector of Crediton, restored a Norman font to the church after it had been thrown out. Torbryan church owes its beautiful fifteenth-century glass and screen to Edward Gosewell who was rector during the Civil War. He whitewashed the screen and buried the glass until after the Restoration. He and his father, who preceded him as rector, are buried in front of the altar.

Another parson who saved church treasures after the Civil War was the Revd James Forbes of Bovey Tracey. He was chaplain to Charles I and to the forces in Germany and the Netherlands and also, like Herrick, accompanied the expedition to the island of Rhé. After the Civil War he was evicted but saved the fifteenth-century brass eagle lectern, according to one account, by burying it in a wild stretch of Bovey Heath or, according to another, by sinking it in a pond. He also secreted the Elizabethan chalice and the registers. He and his treasures returned to the church after the Restoration when he generously presented the church with a pewter alms dish and a flagon.

When the Revd William Willimot arrived at his church of Quethiock, he found it in a dilapidated state and restored it himself, carving the furniture, painting panels of screens and making practically all the stained glass in the church. H. Miles Brown has described Willimot's work on the church and adds that one stained-glass saint has six fingers. Willimot seems to have been a clever craftsman; he made the stained-glass windows in St Paul's church, Penzance, and Gorran Haven, as well as in his own church.

The Revd H. Davis of St Just-in-Roseland gave and placed the stones inscribed with texts along the churchyard path. It was he who took such a pride in the churchyard garden. There were 146 kinds of polyanthus and a variety of other plants, such as palm trees, bamboos and hydrangeas.

Some of the clergy were responsible for building new churches. The new housing estate at Milber, near Newton Abbot, needed a church. The land was bought and a fund started. Then one night the Revd W. Keble

St Just-in-Roseland church

17

The Revd Keble Martin's 'dream church', Milber

Martin, who was looking after the parish for the elderly incumbent, had a strange dream. He found himself preaching in the new church, a most unusual church with three divergent naves in which the congregation could all see the altar which was in front of a rounded apse. The design of the church was so clear to him that he discussed it with his architect brother who agreed that the design was feasible and drew up the plans. These were accepted and the 'dream church' was built.

The Revd William Haslam designed his own church of Baldhu and also St George's church in Truro. Not only did the Revd Robert Aitkin design his church at Pendeen but persuaded his mining congregation to build it. The most famous builder of them all, William of Wykeham, responsible for building much of Winchester Cathedral, was a rector of Menheniot where there is a carving of him on the lectern.

Moreleigh church indirectly owes its existence to a thirteenth-century parson. The unfortunate man, the parson of Woodleigh, was murdered and the church was built by the murderer in expiation of the crime.

Parsons of Devon and Cornwall were also instrumental in the building of secular constructions, such as bridges. Hawker organized the building of King William bridge at Morwenstow. He raised the money by subscriptions and gave a donation himself. King William contributed £20 so the bridge was named after him. Money for bridge building and repairs was raised by some priests by the sale of indulgences. Holne, Camelford, Looe and Staverton bridges were financed in this way, although the Staverton bridge may not have been the present one but a wooden structure (Hemery). The promise of a mass and a dirge encouraged donations for the building of Barnstaple bridge.

John Loveybond, vicar of Egloshayle, was responsible for building Cornwall's longest bridge, the seventeen-arched fifteenth-century bridge at Wadebridge. Four of the arches are now blocked up by the approach roads. It is said that there was difficulty in finding a firm foundation for the piers and that the problem was solved by sinking wool packs. But, as Ravensdale has pointed out, the bridge is built on rock but financed by a wool toll and can therefore be said to be founded on wool. Loveybond's bridge still stands although it has been widened twice.

Bideford bridge or an earlier one on that site is also said to have been built by a priest. A fourteenth-century priest, Sir Richard Gurney, is reported to have had a recurring dream that a bridge was to be built where he saw a large stone on the ground. He saw such a stone by the river and, considering it a heavenly portent, he told his bishop, Grandisson, who instigated the sale of indulgences to pay for and maintain it. So great was the response that some of the money was used for the benefit of Bideford. A wooden chantry bridge with two chapels was built. In the fifteenth century this was replaced by the present stone bridge, though as it was a narrow packhorse bridge it was considerably widened in 1810 and there was a major reconstruction in 1923-5.

Edward Coppleston, Bishop of Llandaff and previously rector of Offwell, built a water-tower to supply his parish. The bishopric was apparently awarded to him for assisting the government on problems of currency and poverty. He tried to remedy the latter in a time of widespread unemployment in his district by building the ornate tower, thus providing both employment and a water supply. Rather unkindly, it was suggested that he built it so that he could survey his diocese and so avoid the need for visiting, but a hill blocked his view.

The Church has always been intimately concerned with learning and has built and maintained many schools. Dr Hawker of Charles' church in Plymouth started both Sunday and day schools for girls, some of whom were clothed by the church. His grandson built the village school at Morwenstow, provided a house for the schoolmaster and maintained the school with very little assistance from others, which eventually proved a drain on his finances. The Revd Frederick Scrivener was instrumental in providing a national school for Gerrans and the Revd William Challoner founded a free school at Braunton.

There is a neat little building in Lustleigh churchyard called the Old Vestry which was originally built by the Revd William Davy as a school. The Revd Jeremiah Trist founded five parish schools. He also built at Veryan some round 'devilscarer' houses at the beginning of the nineteenth century to try to ease the housing shortage at an economical outlay.

Many parsons had to build their own rectories or carry out alterations themselves; this is why some buildings have highly individual features, like the chimneys of Hawker's vicarage at Morwenstow and the famous verse

The school in the churchyard, Lustleigh

One of the round houses at Veryan

which he inscribed over the door. He is supposed to have chosen the site for the vicarage by observing where his sheep lay for shelter. There were some original windows in the Revd Peregrine Arthur Ilbert's rectory at Thurlestone. He had the wheels of his wedding coach made into windows, fitting the space between the spokes with stained glass. He created the rectory, 'Rockhill', out of a barn.

Sir Robert Palk, who was largely responsible for putting Torquay on the map, owned much of the property in the town and built the pier and outer harbour. He had started as a poor curate in Cornwall. However, he was only ordained deacon and gave up his career with the Church to go to India where he made his fortune.

Most parsons took great pride in their churches and spent time and money restoring, renovating and adorning them, even though they were sometimes misguided in their efforts. Some, however, misused or vandalized their churches and appropriated church property.

There was a complaint against the vicar of St Marychurch in 1307 that he not only grazed his beasts in the churchyard and claimed the trees which blew down there, but used the church to make his malt and to store his corn. The congregation were greatly disturbed by the men tramping in and out and leaving the door open so that the ensuing gale which blew around them was enough to lift the roof. Bullocks and pigs were said to have been weighed weekly in the tower of Launceston church at one time.

Baring-Gould was shocked as a boy to see that his grandfather had destroyed a beautiful old screen and benches in Lewtrenchard church, replacing them with deal pews. The deal pulpit that he had installed was mustard yellow with blue hangings, the family's livery colours. Baring-Gould managed to secrete some of the old rood screen so that he was able to have it copied when he took over the living. His daughter, Margaret, did many of the paintings on it. He also replaced the deal pews by more suitable ones, incorporating some old bench-ends and carvings he had rescued.

There are many other instances of rood screens being defaced or removed. Fortunately, in some cases parts of the screens have been rescued and restored.

Churchyards too have been desecrated. At Manaton it was the custom at funeral processions to carry the coffin thrice clockwise round a very fine granite cross in the churchyard. The parson, the Revd C. Carwithen, objected to the custom but was unsuccessful in stopping it, so he secretly smashed the cross.

A number of church possessions seem to have found their way into vicarage gardens. This may have saved some of them from destruction, though that was not always the case. The base of the stone pulpit of St Paul's church, Truro, was used as cricket stumps in the garden of St Clement's vicarage before being rescued and restored to its original use. According to the church guide of South Tawton and South Zeal, an ancient font was retrieved from the old vicarage garden, as was one at Zennor.

Old bench-end in St Peter's church, Lewtrenchard

A seventeenth-century font cover was found in a hen run in 1911. It had been included in the sale of effects of a former rector and was amongst the beehives which were sold. One suspects that the rector had found it a handy substitute for a bee skep. Although in very poor condition it was restored and is now in Zeal Monachorum church.

Lawrence Bodley, canon of Exeter, took books from Exeter Cathedral library and sent them to his brother, Sir Thomas Bodley, in Oxford to help him establish the famous Bodleian library.

CHAPTER FOUR

Eccentric Parsons

LIKE ANY OTHER group of people, the clergy have their fair share of eccentrics. Perhaps the conditions under which they lived encouraged eccentricity. Many were highly educated men, perhaps appointed to some isolated spot in which most of their parishioners were uneducated and living in poverty, the struggle for existence leaving little time for education. Unless they had private means, the parsons were probably impoverished themselves and unable to afford to travel. In the nineteenth century clergy were more autocratic than would be acceptable today and the parishioners were more likely to put up with their eccentricities.

The Revd John Coleridge, vicar of Ottery St Mary and headmaster of the grammar school, was very learned but unbelievably absent-minded and out of touch with reality. He read the Bible in Hebrew to his congregation, most of whom were farm labourers, as he thought they should hear it in the language in which it was written. Unless supervised by his wife, he would wear his clean shirts on top of his dirty ones.

Daphne du Maurier mentions two Cornish parsons who were certainly eccentric. One, a widower, housed his daughters with the poultry in a barn. Until they were taken into care as teenagers they were complete strangers to the normal life around them.

The other parson turned nights into days and knocked up his parishioners for a friendly chat (on his part!) at various times during the night. He played the church organ in the early hours of the morning. His sister was with him (he was a bachelor) and she slept through the recital in one of the church pews.

A. L. Rowse describes another Cornish cleric who would have nothing to do with his church. When occasionally a parson came to take a service for him, he would not attend despite his patrons pleading for him to do so as an example to his parishioners. They would see him standing at his garden gate in his flowered dressing-gown and smoking his hookah. Despite such eccentric behaviour and neglect of his parish, he could not be removed from his living or from his rectory.

One of the strangest clergymen was a curate in Cornwall, mentioned by Goodenough. This curate was so crazy that he had to be tethered to the altar rails or reading desk. He supplemented his income by playing his violin in public houses.

William Botrell gives an amusing account of another eccentric, Parson Spry, curate of Sennen and St Levan in the 1820s. He neglected both his clerical duties and his church; he would not go to church at all if the weather was bad. He wore the most extraordinary unecclesiastical clothes. Once he was seen walking the streets of Plymouth in a kind of sailor suit made of striped ticking. Nevertheless his parishioners liked him as he was so good humoured and his eccentricities amused them.

They would certainly never forget his velocipede. He acquired it as an economy since, like most parsons of his day, he was poorly paid and could not afford to keep a horse or even to hire one for the travelling involved in his parish work. The velocipede could reach a fair speed downhill, so Spry offered to race farmers down Tultuf Hill for a bet on market day. He always won as the horses were so terrified of his contraption that they shied and threw their riders and even jumped the hedge to escape from it.

He was not so lucky when racing down a steep hill near Alverton. He lost control and careered down to the bottom and into Alverton Water where women with market baskets full of butter, eggs and other farm produce were watering their horses. He crashed into the middle of them, frightening the horses which threw the women and scattered their wares. The women were furious and set on him, throwing their ruined produce at him and rolling him in the mud; eventually some men had to come to his rescue. The following Sunday a large congregation gathered at the foot of a nearby hill to witness Spry's arrival with the velocipede. However, he was too ill to go to church. By the next Sunday he had regained his health and courage, but strangely only his dog, Sport, arrived at the foot of the hill. Sport led the people to where his master, plastered in mud, was just crawling out of a pond. His velocipede was still in the pond!

Unlike Parson Spry, the Revd Frederick William Densham was certainly not popular with his parishioners. He was incumbent from 1931 to 1935 at Warleggan on the edge of Bodmin Moor. His unpopularity was perhaps partly due to his long sojourn abroad which had made him lose touch with normal living conditions in the parish.

Daphne du Maurier in *Living Cornwall* describes how, when Densham came to tea with her parents, he enquired if they knew of a gardener; he said that he would pay him at the rate of one penny a year plus potatoes. He did succeed in acquiring an organist, but the poor fellow escaped shortly after his arrival, having been locked in a bedroom furnished only with a packing case and a pile of sacks.

The friction between Densham and his flock was so bad that he surrounded his vicarage with a high barbed-wire fence and kept fierce half-starved dogs to discourage intrusion. Groceries and post were left at the gate. Even his manservant had to ask permission to enter the house.

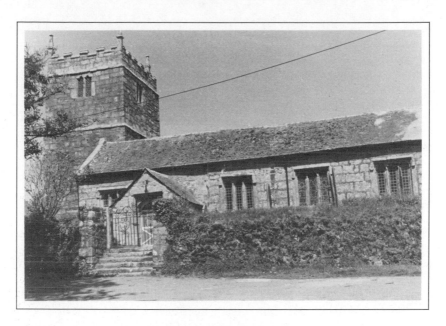

Warleggan church

According to James Turner, the parson closed the Sunday school and further angered the parishioners by threatening to sell the organ which was bought as a First World War memorial. He made an island by digging a moat round a piece of land and also created a children's playground near the village hall, but no child came to play in it. He never visited in the parish.

People refused to attend Densham's services. He must have resented preaching to an empty church because he propped cardboard and wooden models of people labelled with the names of previous vicars in the pews. The angry parishioners eventually complained about him to their bishop. The bishop visited Warleggan and had a meeting with Densham, but was unable to turn him out as he had not transgressed ecclesiastical law. Then one day, as nothing had been seen of the vicar and he had not appeared to let his servant in, the door of the vicarage was forced open. The vicar was found dead at the foot of the stairs. The place was littered with paper and rubbish and the floor boards had been torn up for firewood.

The Revd Leighton Sandys Wason certainly qualifies to be included amongst the eccentrics. His friend, the Revd Bernard Walke, said that he was a most unworldly man. Born in 1867, he went to Westminster School and Christchurch, Oxford. He became parson of Cury and Gunwalloe in Cornwall. Like Walke, he had very strong Catholic leanings and even said mass in Latin. He was deprived of his living but would not leave, until

27

eventually a group of farmers threw him out. His belongings were piled on to wagons, and Wason, his cousin, his gardener and family, and a dog all descended on the Walkes one night. They also inadvertently brought with them the remains of the invasion of caterpillars which had overrun the vicarage! Wason then lost interest in the flit and settled down to a game of chess, leaving the others to store his furniture.

On an earlier occasion, when Wason heard that Walke was ill he sent a telegram to inform him that he would say mass for him at 10.30 the next morning. The next day Walke received another telegram: Wason had over-slept and had not said mass but promised to do so the following day!

On one occasion the Walkes were invited to dinner with Wason. When they knocked at the door there was no answer. Eventually he appeared from the garden with his arms full of iris muttering that the colour scheme was wrong but otherwise ignoring them as he went in and shut the door. There was another long wait during which they banged on the door. Wason looked out from an upstairs window and said that the table was wrong without a black centre and that he was looking for his hat. After another long wait he finally opened the door and warmly welcomed them as though they had just arrived. His tall hat filled with iris was the centre-piece of his dining table.

Among the eccentric parsons of Devon and Cornwall, one of the first who comes to mind is Robert Stephen Hawker. He was born in Plymouth in 1834. His father was a medical man who later turned to the Church; when his father left Plymouth to take up his curacy, young Stephen remained with his grandfather who was rector of Charles' Church, Plymouth. Judging from all the pranks that the boy played, his grandfather must often have wished that the family had taken him with them.

Whilst still an undergraduate at Oxford, he married Charlotte I'ans, a talented and attractive woman much older than he was. It seems to have been a singularly happy marriage. His first post after ordination was as curate to North Tamerton. He then moved to Morwenstow, which living, along with the curacy of Welcombe in Devon, he held until his death.

His dress was eccentric: he wore a fisherman's jersey with a red cross on it where the sword entered Christ's body, a three-quarter-length plum-coloured coat, a brown, pink or black hat and red gloves. When it was cold he topped his ensemble with a yellow poncho made from a blanket.

Hawker originated the custom of harvest festival. Many of his fellow clergymen were opposed to it, but it became so popular that it was adopted by other churches throughout the country. The offertory was also his innovation. His services were original. Sometimes he prostrated himself flat on his face on the floor, his arms outstretched. The floor of his church was none too clean either as he scattered it with herbs which were not changed regularly. His curate once took two barrow-loads of dirt and rubbish from the church. Hawker took out the lower panels of the pulpit as he thought the congregation had a right to see the parson's feet.

The Revd R. S. Hawker at the age of sixty

Hawker's birthplace: 6 Norley Street, Plymouth

The figurehead from the Caledonia *in Morwenstow churchyard*

In later life his addiction to opium, which he started taking as medicine, may have been responsible for some of his eccentric behaviour, but there is no doubt that some of his eccentricity was contrived to impress tourists. His first wife's death was a terrible blow to him and increased his dependence on opium. The dreadful shipwrecks on that notoriously dangerous coast near Morwenstow worried Hawker greatly when he helped to search for the often badly mangled bodies washed up on the shore. This added to his nervous strain and his reliance on the drug. He buried all the victims of the shipwrecks in his churchyard; the figurehead of the wrecked *Caledonia* that he placed there still stands guard over the captain's grave and those of her crew.

When he married his second wife, Pauline Kuczynski, he tried to overcome the addiction. Three daughters were born to them and although he was very fond and proud of them they greatly increased his financial worries. Just before his death in 1875 he became a member of the Catholic Church.

The Revd H. Miles Brown cites another eccentric, Sir Harry Trelawny, who was the parson of St Allen and later of Egloshayle in Cornwall. He emulated the Vicar of Bray. When he was at Looe he was a Presbyterian minister. In 1781 he was ordained in the Church of England, but later became a Catholic and finally a Catholic priest in 1830.

CHAPTER FIVE

Literature

MOST PARSONS IN Devon and Cornwall were well educated and many had travelled both in Britain and on the continent. They had a good deal of writing to do in the course of their duties, so it is therefore not surprising to find a number of authors amongst them. Some, in isolated country parishes with little in the way of entertainment, no doubt wrote as a pleasurable way of passing the time. Others wished to put some message across to the public, some wrote to eke out a meagre stipend and perhaps a few wrote from the human failing of wanting to see their names in print.

Several clergy had collections of their sermons printed, among them Sydney Smith, Kingsley, Davy and Prince. Many theological books and papers were written by the clergy, as might be expected.

Perhaps one of the most prolific writers of ecclesiastical works was the Revd W. Davy. He was rather a pathetic character and should probably never have been a parson. His talent was for mechanics and he had an inventive mind.

He was born in 1743 in the parish of Tavistock, attended Exeter Grammar School and went on to Balliol College, Oxford. After ordination he went to Morctonhampstead and whilst there married. He moved to Drewsteignton and then to Lustleigh as curate-in-charge. The stipend at Lustleigh was only £40 and he had to pay £5 for the rectory rent. Davy published six volumes of his sermons but because his subscribers defaulted he lost £100. His farming venture also failed, through his complete lack of experience.

No one would publish his long work, *General System of Theology*, so he decided to publish it himself. With the help of his servant he did so — all twenty-six volumes of about 500 pages each. His lack of money increased the problems: first he had to make a printing-press and then he could afford to buy only enough type to print four pages at a time. When the first volume was completed he sent copies to the universities, to the Dean and Chapter and the Archdeacon of Exeter. Some never even acknowledged the book and those who did offered no help or encouragement.

He had to move into a small farmhouse because he could not afford the expenses incurred by the large rectory; there he devoted much time and loving care to his garden. In 1825 he was given the living of Winkleigh, but by then he was too old to benefit from the change and was upset at having to leave his beloved garden which must have given him some consolation for his lack of literary success. The new vicarage was damp and he caught a cold and died the following year.

The first book to be printed in Exeter was written by the Revd Thomas Fuller. He was born in 1608 in Northamptonshire and after taking orders and serving in several parishes he lived for two years in Exeter during the Civil War when Charles I was there and became his chaplain. His book, for which he is chiefly remembered, was called *Worthies of England and Good Thoughts in Bad Times*.

As would be expected, there were a number of hymn writers among the Devon and Cornish parsons, but perhaps more surprisingly, some also wrote secular poetry. One of the earliest of these poets was Joseph of Exeter, who lived in the twelfth century. Herrick is of course the best known of these parson poets.

Robert Herrick was born in 1591 in Goldsmiths' Row, Cheapside. His father had moved to London from Leicestershire as he wanted to be a goldsmith. Robert, one of eight children, was only a year old when his father made a will and two days later fell from their fourth-floor window on to the street and was fatally injured. In those days, the property of a suicide went to the Crown. Although suicide was suspected it could not be proved and, moreover, the family on both sides had influential connections. Therefore eventually his possessions were distributed according to his will, one third to his wife and the rest divided amongst the six children then living. One died young and the youngest was born posthumously.

There is a gap in our knowledge of Herrick's early life. It might have been spent at Hampton on the Thames where Robert's mother had a married sister. He was apprenticed as a goldsmith to his uncle, Sir William Herrick, who had served his own apprenticeship with Robert's father. It was during this period of his life that Robert wrote his first poems. After a time he concluded that a career as a goldsmith has no appeal for him and when he was released by his uncle he went to St John's College, Cambridge. Later, for economy, he transferred to Trinity Hall where he studied law. Whilst at Cambridge he met John Weeks, who was to become a lifelong friend. He also became a Devon parson.

After graduation he was ordained a deacon and the next day a priest. Little is known of his life between ordination and taking up the living in Dean Prior, but he is thought to have spent time in London where he mixed with men of culture and where he met Ben Jonson whom he revered. He was also becoming quite well known for his poetry. It is known that he was the Duke of Buckingham's chaplain on the expedition to the island of Rhé. In 1628 Herrick was given the living of Dean Prior which may have been in recognition of his services as chaplain on the expedition. He was installed as vicar in 1630.

Robert Herrick: the portrait published in Hesperides

Life could not have been easy at Dean Prior at first. His predecessor, a puritan, was popular with the local people and it must have been difficult for Herrick, the ardent royalist, to follow him. Country folk are conservative and not fond of change and a new parson from the big city may not have been the type they would have chosen. Herrick must have been very sad to leave the life and culture of London and sorry to part with his friends.

Today traffic roars along the Plymouth–Exeter dual carriageway right beneath the walls of Dean Prior vicarage, now much altered. In Herrick's day the church and vicarage were isolated and he could have had little in common with the peasants who formed most of his congregation. He no doubt appreciated the company of his sister-in-law who came to keep house for him until she died. Whatever the disappointments that Dean Prior may have held for him, it seems to have inspired him to write some of his best poetry, poetry which gives us glimpses of his life there, his home, his pets, the locals and the festivals.

He sometimes visited London, although he was not supposed to do so without dispensation from his bishop. There are indications that an illegitimate child of Thomasin Parsons was his. Her father was a musical friend of Herrick's and he stayed with the family on a visit to London.

Herrick was turned out of his parish by the puritans in 1648. Perhaps he was not sorry for it meant he could go back to his beloved London. How he lived is not known but he had influential relatives and patrons. During his exile *Hesperides*, a volume of poems, was published; it contains the only known portrait of him.

He was reinstated when Charles I came to the throne. Patience Baldwin, his former housekeeper for whom he later wrote a charming epitaph, came to look after him again. He was sixty-nine when he returned and lived to be eighty-three. It is not known where in the church or churchyard he was buried, but from one of his poems we learn that he wished to be buried outside the church, perhaps amongst the flowers he loved.

Hawker's poem 'The Western Men', which we hear today roared by football crowds is certainly his best-known poem though not his best. He first published it anonymously and people thought that it was an ancient poem. The refrain is old but the rest is Hawker's composition. He published one book of poems, *Tendrils*, whilst still a boy. Later he published collections of his poems, *Records of the Western Shore*, *Ecclesia* which was reprinted with additional material as *Reeds Shaken by the Wind*, *Cornish Ballads* and his best, the unfinished *The Quest of Sangraal*. It is interesting to learn that he met Tennyson when the latter was in Cornwall collecting material for his great Arthurian poem. Few people read Hawker's poems now.

The Revd John Woolcot wrote popular odes. Born at Dodbrook in 1738 and brought up by his uncle, a doctor in Truro, he also became a doctor. He went to Jamaica and took orders as a clergyman but when he left there he seems to have reverted to his former profession. His odes about the famous of his day were popular and earned him a good income but they were coarse and often cruel and could hardly be described as poetry.

One parson owed his profession to a poem. The Revd Benjamin Kennicott, son of the parish clerk, was born in Totnes in 1718 and attended the grammar school there. His sister was lady's maid to Mrs Elizabeth Courtney and when the lady nearly died from eating a poisonous herb in mistake for watercress, he wrote a poem on her recovery addressed to her and her husband. She was so struck by the poem that she organized a subscription to send Kennicott to Wadham College, Oxford. He fully justified his patron's confidence in his ability by gaining B.A., M.A. and D.D. degrees. He was rector of Culham (which living he later relinquished in order to study), a prebendary of Westminster and canon of Christchurch. His contribution to sacred literature was a collection of texts from the Hebrew Bible in two volumes.

Professor Hoskins in *Devon* has written of a parson of Plymtree, the Revd Thomas Mozley who, for several years wrote the leader for *The Times*. The subject on which he was to write was sent from London to the local station every afternoon and he dispatched the finished leader later the same afternoon.

Letter writing was an important part of the life of a nineteenth-century parson, particularly important to those in isolated parishes where letters were one of the few contacts with the outside world. Perhaps for this reason they kept them to read over and over again. Many of these letters have been collected and published, and give us an interesting glimpse not only into the parsons' lives but into the life of the times. Kingsley's wife, Fanny, published his — suitably edited — letters and many of Hawker's are included in the biography written by his son-in-law, Byles.

Books on a variety of subjects, such as campanology, sport, archaeology, travel, natural history, philosophy and history, have come from the pens of Devonshire and Cornish parsons.

The Revd William Keble Martin is well known for his illustrations of wild flowers. He began these at Oxford when fellow students complained of the difficulty of identifying flowers from written descriptions. He met the distinguished botanist Dr Druce who later sent him rare flowers from all over the British Isles. His first drawing for the book was of a snowdrop with ivy leaves and was done in 1899 at Dartington where his father was rector.

After various posts in the north of England Keble Martin moved to the parish of Haccombe with Coffinswell. Life was more leisurely there and he was able to make good progress with his flower paintings. He also wrote a short history of Coffinswell. However, additional parochial work which he took on to help the elderly rector at Milber subsequently took up much of his spare time and he had little to give to his painting. Moreover, some of the original ones on poor quality paper had become discoloured with age, and had to be done again. In 1934 he became vicar of Great Torrington. Once again his spare time was very limited and his output of paintings suffered.

After ten years at Great Torrington he was offered the living of Combeinteignhead with Milber. He had been responsible for the building of a new church at Milber, but there were complaints that it should not have been built, so he felt that he should accept the living to face these accusations. However, he found the travelling involved, particularly in winter, very difficult. He could not get an easier parish so at seventy-two he retired to Gidleigh and later Woodbury. He now had plenty of time for painting. He also studied at the British Museum's herbarium and visited Kew and the Natural History Museum.

His flower paintings were exhibited at a Royal Horticultural Society meeting and he tried to find a publisher for them. Finally he collected signatures in an appeal for funds and raised £1000. His wife wrote to the Duke of Edinburgh who asked to see the paintings. The Duke was a great

37

help in getting them published and wrote the foreword to the book. The book became a best seller. Keble Martin appeared on television, was nominated author of the year by Hatchard's, received an honorary degree from Exeter University and met numerous people who called to have their copies of the book signed.

As many parsons stayed in one parish for a long time and were therefore familiar with the surrounding area, it is not surprising that some wrote descriptions of the topography or of the natural history of the countryside around them. The Revd Hugh Breton wrote *The Heart of Dartmoor*. The Revd Richard Polwhele not only wrote on ancient customs and produced many volumes of histories of Devon and Cornwall but was a theologian, chronicler and noted poet as well. He was born in 1760 and served in parishes in Devon (Kenton) and Cornwall (Manaccan, near Helston, Newlyn East and St Anthony-in-Meneage). Samuel Rowe (1793-1853), a former bookseller and the rector of Crediton wrote many guide books on Devon, and the Revd John Pike (1790-1857) wrote a guide to the scenery in the neighbourhood of Ashburton where he was born and also wrote on the botany and antiquities of Devon. Many other parsons wrote about their churches and parishes.

The Revd J. Prince is well known for his *Worthies of Devon*. He was born at Axminster in 1643 and was an ancestor of Winston Churchill. He was vicar of Berry Pomeroy for forty-two years. The Revd Robert Burscough of Totnes allowed Prince to use his comprehensive library which must have helped him considerably with his writing. *Worthies of Devon* is based on a transcript by Sir William Pole, and is a collection of verse on the notable families of the county.

Sydney Smith was noted both as a wit and an essayist. He was born in 1771. His father was quite affluent but a mean and difficult man who must have caused a good deal of misery amongst his family. His mother was daughter of a Huguenot refugee. Sydney was one of five children of the marriage.

His schooling began at six when he was sent to Southampton. Later with one of his brothers, he went to Winchester where life was very hard and he hated it. The food was so poor and in such short supply that Sydney, ever resourceful even in his youth, made a catapult to try to bag a turkey to make a substantial meal.

After gaining a degree at Oxford Smith was ordained and took up a post as a private tutor. Writing began to take up much of his spare time. He published six of his sermons and then, as they were well received, a second volume containing six more. He was one of the founders of the Edinburgh Review and its first editor as well as a regular contributor.

After giving up the post as tutor, he went to London where he was appointed to two evening preacherships and gave a number of lectures on moral philosophy, some of which were later published posthumously. He became friendly with Lord and Lady Holland who greatly influenced him.

Friends helped him to the living of Foston-le-Clay, between York and

Malton. At first he continued to live in London but the Archbishop of York insisted that he take charge of the parish himself. His two volumes of sermons paid for the move, first to a rented house and later to one he built in the parish.

Despite his numerous duties as a parson and those involving his work as a magistrate, his enthusiastic farming of the glebe land and the education of his children, he still found time to write for the Edinburgh Review. He loved his family and kept the children amused by stories which he made up for them. When he was working, writing or reading, he always sat with the family, quite unperturbed by the chatter and movement around him. His ready wit and good-natured chuckle kept the family and staff laughing too.

Later Smith was appointed a prebendary of Bristol with the living of Halberton in Devon, which gave a boost to his finances and after receiving several legacies he eventually became a very rich man. He was able to change the living of Foston-le-Clay for that of Combe Florey in Somerset where his nephew became his curate. A further appointment was conferred on him, that of canon residentiary of St Paul's.

Sabine Baring-Gould, known for his folk-song collection, had a most unusual childhood. His father, Captain Edward Baring-Gould, had held a commission in the East India Company and had been invalided home after a driving accident. He had married and lived for a time in Bratton Clovelly, but he had a restless nature and spent years trailing round Europe with his family. Sabine's schooling was neglected, being limited to two years as a boarder at King's College, London and one year as a day boy at Warwick Grammar School, and even then he was ill for much of the time. Between the ages of three and sixteen he had spent only three years in England. Consequently he was a good linguist, speaking five languages fluently, and he had many interests. He went to Cambridge as a classical scholar but his lack of schooling, and hence grounding in the classics, had left its mark and he achieved only a pass degree. His first published work of fiction dates from his college days. During the holidays he roamed Dartmoor, fascinated by its antiquities and natural history. He also visited old churches and the small inns where old men sang folk songs.

He was very devout: he had joined the Tractarian Movement and wanted to enter the Church. His father, however, did not approve, considering that one of his younger sons should be ordained instead. He tried to persuade Sabine to teach at Malborough Grammar School where his uncle was the headmaster, but he would not and instead taught in the choir school of St Barnaby's in Pimlico to try to learn something of the lives of ordinary working-class people. There was no pay, only food and lodgings. Eventually a friend found him a post as an assistant master at a Woodward School in Sussex. He remained there for eight years.

When neither of the younger brothers wanted to enter the church, his father relented and Sabine was ordained. He was appointed curate at Horbury, Yorkshire, where he was given a section of the parish to look

Lew House

after. He rented a cottage and started a night school and services in a small chapel he made there. It was a great success and soon larger premises had to be built. It was during his Horbury curacy that he wrote the famous hymn 'Onward! Christian Soldiers'. It was there also that he met his future wife, Grace Taylor, a mill girl. She was very young and before they were married he sent her to a woman relative of his to be educated. There were fifteen children of the marriage.

Just before he married he moved to Dalton in Yorkshire and was then offered a living in Mersea, Essex where they lived for ten years. They disliked the cold damp area, but it was there that Sabine wrote what is probably his best novel *Mehalah*, as well as *The Lives of the Saints* in sixteen volumes. Unfortunately, as the publishers went into bankruptcy, he was not fully paid for his exhausting labour.

On the death of his uncle Baring-Gould moved to Lewtrenchard and took over the living of which he had the advowson. He kept a curate for the very small parish of 200 parishioners and this enabled him to supervise the running of his estate and to write.

He had frequent worries over money which were increased by his lack of ability in financial affairs and by his bursts of extravagance. He used to have to ask his bank manager if he had enough money to pay his bills. The reconstruction of Lew House, the building of the new rectory and estate cottages, the restoration of the church, foreign travel, books, antiques, paintings and, not least, the expenses of his large family and the staff required to run such a large house all needed a considerable income. He tried to remain solvent by writing a novel a year. He did not give his family an expensive education. As soon as the boys were old enough they had to be self-supporting.

A debt we owe Baring-Gould is for his collections of folk songs. He collected many songs from the West Country, writing down the songs people sang to him. In this he was greatly helped by Dr F.W. Bussell and the Revd H. Fleetwood, both good musicians. Dr Bussell was very eccentric. He had a high conveyance made so that he could see over the hedges as he rode along. The vehicle was fitted with bookshelf, table, lamp and a case for liquor. When at Lewtrenchard, he had hot-house flowers sent for buttonholes to match his exotic ties. Baring-Gould and his colleagues altered some of the earthy words to the songs to make them fit for publication. The songs they collected were published under the editorship of Cecil Sharp as *Songs of the West*.

Baring-Gould wrote several books on Dartmoor, its antiquities and local characters, as well as biography, history and Christian theology, of which *The Church Revival* is notable.

His wife, Grace, ran the household of about thirty people, plus numerous guests, smoothly and efficiently. Sadly, towards the end of her life she became a complete cripple. Her death was a great blow to her husband, as the Latin inscription on her tombstone shows: 'Half my life'. When Baring-Gould died in 1924 there were so many people at his funeral that they could not all get in the church.

When one thinks of novels written by Devonshire parsons, the name of Charles Kingsley always comes to mind. Yet he was not really a Devonshire parson in that he never had a parish in the county. He is, however, included here as he was born in Devon, spent part of his childhood in his father's parish of Clovelly, returned to the county several times to recuperate from illness and always regarded himself as a Devon man.

Charles Kingsley was born in the vicarage (since demolished) at Holne where his father, also Charles, was a temporary curate in charge. His mother was of a family of sugar planters in Barbados. Shortly after Charles was born they moved from one temporary curacy to another and then to Barnack where the child developed nervous trouble which affected him throughout most of his life and left him with a stutter. The family went to Ilfracombe and then to Clovelly and it was here that Charles developed his great love of Devon which he never lost.

His happy life in Clovelly ended when his father took the living of St Luke's, Chelsea. While there, for a holiday, his father had exchanged duties with a parson from Checkendon in Oxfordshire. Charles went to stay there on vacation and met Frances (Fanny) Grenfell. He and Fanny immediately felt a strong bond between them. They corresponded when he returned to Cambridge and the friendship ripened into love, but her family (her parents were dead) were strongly opposed to her marrying Charles.

Fanny had strong religious convictions and she influenced Charles in deciding to enter the Church. He obtained a curacy at Eversley. As Fanny

Charles Kingsley

was adamant that she would marry Kingsley or no one, her family relented and they were married. When the living at Eversley became vacant he was made vicar.

Kingsley had been deeply influenced by F. D. Maurice and identified himself with the Chartist Movement. Together with Maurice and Ludlow, a barrister, he started a penny periodical, *Politics for the People*, to which he contributed under the name of 'Parson Lot'. In addition to his parish work, he took up a part-time post teaching literature at Queen's College for Women. As a result of his Chartist activities and his compassion for the poor, he wrote the novels *Yeast*, *Alton Locke* and *Hypatia* which caused an outcry and resulted in attacks in the press.

During a visit to Torquay, for the benefit of his wife's health, he indulged his interest for natural history. He collected specimens in Tor Bay and as a result of his studies wrote *Glaucus*, a book on marine life for children. He had hoped to preach in Torquay but was not permitted to do so because of his reputation as an author of controversial novels.

After leaving Torquay, the Kingsleys went to Bideford where they rented Northdown House (now part of Stella Maris Convent School). While there Kingsley published *Westward Ho!* The book was a great success and provided a useful income since during the stay at Torquay and Bideford expenses had been heavy. He wrote another novel at Bideford, *Two Years Ago*, but it was not so successful, nor was a later one, *Hereward the Wake*.

The Prince Consort invited Kingsley to preach at Buckingham Palace and he was appointed royal chaplain. The royal favour mitigated the attacks by the press which his earlier novels had caused. His post as professor of modern history at Cambridge was due to Prince Albert's help and he was appointed one of the tutors of the Prince of Wales.

One of the best known of Kingsley's books is *The Water Babies*. The fireplace in his study at Eversley had steps inside the chimney for the child sweeps to climb. He referred to the plight of these children in a sermon he preached before the queen. Kingsley's concern in this matter was instrumental in bringing about the Chimney Sweeps Regulation Act.

A lecture tour of America accompanied by his elder daughter, Rose, taxed his failing health. He was not well when he returned and caught a cold which turned to pneumonia, causing his death in 1875.

His wife survived another sixteen years; she wrote memoirs of his life and edited his letters. Of his four children — two boys and two girls — the younger daughter was a novelist and Rose wrote a book on her travels with her father.

Several of the Cornish and Devonshire parsons wrote hymns for their churches, perhaps for some special occasion. A few, such as the Revd Francis Lyte, were able to set them to music themselves, others wrote only the words.

Practically everyone knows 'Rock of Ages' and the belief that its writer was inspired to write it after sheltering from a storm in a cleft of rock in the

43

Mendips. Not so many know that the author was the Revd Augustus Montague Toplady or could tell you anything of his life. He was born at Farnham in Surrey and attended Westminster School. His father, a major, was killed in the siege of Cartagena and the boy later went with his mother to live in Ireland. There he entered Trinity College, Dublin, was ordained and appointed to a curacy at Blagdon in Somerset. Later the living of Harpford with Venn Ottery was obtained for him. This he exchanged for Broadhembury. He wrote on Calvanistic themes, his best book being *The Historic Proof of Doctrinal Calvinism in the Church of England in 1774*. In his writings he viciously attacked Wesley.

Although Toplady continued to hold Broadhembury until his death, he was non-resident after consumption forced him to move to London where he died of the disease in 1778. There are memorials to him in both Harpford and Broadhembury. Other hymns he wrote are 'A sovereign protection I have' and 'Object of my first desire'.

Probably the best-known hymn to come from the West Country is 'Abide with me'. It is as familiar to football crowds as it is to church congregations. The author, Henry Francis Lyte, wrote a number of hymns, including 'God of mercy, God of grace', 'Pleasant are thy courts above' and 'Praise, my soul, the King of heaven'.

Lyte was born near Kelso in Scotland in 1793. His father was a feckless man who maintained that he had never married Lyte's mother. The couple eventually parted, the mother taking the youngest son with her and the father the two elder boys. The father, who was in the army, sent the boys to Portora Royal School in Enniskillen. Francis was brilliant, but his brother was dull and was returned to his father who had not paid the school fees. The headmaster kept Francis at the school and became his guardian. Lyte entered Trinity College, Dublin where he studied medicine until he felt strongly drawn to the Church.

After ordination Lyte went to Taghmon near Wexford and there he suffered his first attack of the chest ailment which was to trouble him all his life. His next post was a lectureship at Marazion where he was technically a curate. There he married Ann Maxwell who was a Methodist and remained so after her marriage. Lyte's father-in-law made him an allowance which was of considerable help to the young couple. The climate around Marazion did not suit Lyte and they moved to Sway in the New Forest where their first daughter was born and died. He wrote much of his poetry here but probably had no permanent post. Their next move was to Dittisham where again he had no full-time post. Here their second daughter was born. Lyte did temporary duty at the chapel of ease at Lower Brixham and was asked by the congregation to become their permanent minister, but as he could not find a suitable house, he went to Charlton to take over a parish during the vicar's absence.

He finally moved to Brixham in 1824, officially as minister incumbent. At first he rented a house in Burton Street then later moved to Berry Head House, a former military hospital, and bought 21 acres of land on the head.

Burton Court Flats, formerly Burton House, home of the Revd Francis Lyte

In his later years he was dogged by ill health and had to spend the winters in the warmer climate of southern Europe. These journeys, together with the cost of a university education for three sons and the upkeep of a large house and an extensive library, added financial worry to that of his health and the anxiety caused by the loss of members of his congregation to the Dissenters. He died in Nice on one of his journeys south.

Lyte's famous hymn, 'Abide with me', was not written, as tradition has it, after watching a beautiful sunset shortly before preaching his last sermon in England. He probably started it when he was in Cornwall or just before he went there and kept adding to it and altering it until just before his death. It is said that W.H. Monk composed the tune to it in ten minutes.

CHAPTER SIX

Sporting Parsons

AT ONE TIME Devon was noted for its hunting parsons. When Bishop Phillpotts came to Exeter, practically all the parsons in his diocese spent at least one day a week hunting and twenty of them kept their own packs of hounds. Phillpotts disapproved of his clergy hunting but could not stop them. One old West Country clergyman announced in church the meets of the stag hounds and fox hunting notices were frequently given from the pulpit. Another is said to have preached to his congregation of sportsmen, after they had sung the hymn 'As pants the hart for cooling streams', a sermon on 'Lo, we heard of it at Ephratah, and we found it in the wood'.

Probably in many of the parishes with hunting parsons the parishioners did not suffer. The Revd Jack Russell, for all his hunting, still had his parishioners at heart. He kept a curate to minister to their needs if he were not there and was a much-loved parson. However, in some parishes the sport interfered with the parsons' parochial duties. When the Revd John Boyce, incumbent of Sherwell, wanted to hunt on Sunday, the clerk put a notice on the church door to say that the service had been cancelled as the 'master' had gone stag hunting with 'Sir Thomas' (Ackland). One Devon parson found that church services kept him away from his sport, so he closed his church for three months each year while he enjoyed the shooting season.

Some parsons got into trouble for their hunting. An example is Thomas Flemming, rector of South Molton, who, in 1328, hunted in the park of the Bishop of Exeter at Bishop's Nympton. He had a good bag, for, with his own pack of dogs supplemented by others, he killed 200 animals. Not only did he hunt in the bishop's park, but he stole animal troughs, wooden benches, several bullocks, carts and other things. He was lucky to escape excommunication by payment of a hundred marks to Bishop Grandisson.

The Revd Thomas Granger went on a fox shoot with some local farmers. Had they restricted themselves to foxes there would have been no trouble as foxes were considered vermin and anyone who killed one was paid 10 s. Unfortunately they 'accidently' shot a hare and a local man informed the Justice of Peace who fined them £5. However, they recovered the money by confiscating the awards that the informer would have earned for fox killing, until sufficient foxes had been handed in to pay for the fine.

Probably one of the most widely known of all the Devonshire and Cornish parsons is Jack Russell. Everyone has heard of Jack Russell terriers, the breed he originated. His ancestor was John Russell who established the family in Devon when he was sent to quell the Prayer-book Rebellion and left relatives behind to maintain the peace.

John ('Jack') Russell was born in 1795. His father, a parson, moved from Iddesleigh to a curacy at Dartmouth and then moved again to Callington when Jack was still less than two years old. Jack probably got his love of hunting from his father who hunted and kept a pack of hounds and took paying pupils to pay for them. His pupils were very hard working as the prize for the best pupil during the week was the use of a pony for the day's hunting.

After graduation and ordination, Jack Russell was appointed to the curacy of George Nympton (formerly Nymet St George) and was also responsible for weekly duty at South Molton. He married Penelope Bury, daughter of Admiral Bury of Dennington, Swimbridge. It was an ideal marriage as they were devoted to each other and she shared her husband's love of hunting and was an excellent horsewoman. Soon after his marriage, Russell went as curate to his father at Iddesleigh. Their first child died whilst very young but later a son, Bury, was born to them. He also proved to be a good huntsman when he grew up.

Penelope's cousin then offered Russell the living of Swimbridge with Landkey which he accepted. Here he kept a pack of hounds and also hunted with other packs, including the 'Let 'em Alones' of his friend Templer of Stover. The pack was so-called because the dogs were not allowed to kill the foxes; instead, the foxes were kept in two yards to use for future hunts. When they hunted, Templer's pet monkey went along too, strapped on a horse.

Russell bought his first terrier, Trump, from a milkman in Oxford when he was a student there. Later he was much in demand as a judge at dog shows.

Although Russell hunted so much he did not neglect his clerical duties. He was a good preacher and he and his wife were always ready to help anyone in trouble, but he never visited unless asked to do so. He was very popular not only with the villagers but also with the gypsies whom he allowed to stay on his land. He always got on well with the Nonconformists, unlike some of his fellow clergymen. One of his curates, E.W.L. Davies, also a huntsman, wrote his biography.

In 1879 Russell was offered the living of Black Torrington. The living was worth £500, which was more than that of Swimbridge and, though leaving Swimbridge was a sad parting for him, Russell needed the money. Probably his son had had financial help from him. Bury had been in the army but gave it up and became a bank manager. At one period he became a bankrupt. He died shortly after his father's death. Russell was also

47

The Revd John Russell

hospitable and generous and his hounds and hunting must have cost quite a large sum.

When he died in 1883, the crowd at his funeral was so large that about a thousand people had to stand in the churchyard as they could not get into the church.

John Froude, with whom Russell hunted, followed his father as vicar of Knowstone cum Molland. It was a valuable living and he had a considerable private fortune. He was a well-educated man, a graduate of Oxford and a relation of the gifted Froudes of Dartington, but something seems to have gone very wrong with his life. Some said that it was because he was thwarted in love. The superstitious even said his power for evil was because he grew mandrake in his garden. Blackmore was inspired to put him in his book *The Maid of Sker* as Parson Chowne. This was perhaps because he was present when Froude, after running a fox to earth which he had hunted over Knowstone Moor, remarked somewhat flippantly that he would have to leave to conduct a burial service for which he was already an hour late. He neglected his parochial duties and took services only when it suited him and then the church was empty.

Froude was a very good huntsman and kept a pack of hounds. Although an accomplished rider and no doubt able to judge a horse, his horse dealing methods were despicable. One customer was plied with drink until he was so drunk that Froude succeeded in selling him a blind horse.

The villagers were afraid of him and credited him with having the evil eye. It was said that if he did not get what he wanted their crops might be ruined or their ricks fired or the wheels of their vehicles tampered with to cause an accident. If someone bought a horse which Froude wanted, hempseed was sometimes put into its eye so that the poor creature was in agony and threw its rider. The vandals who caused all the trouble were not paid by him but he provided them with food, bed and a fire at his house, though if they were caught he never defended them.

He himself did not escape retribution and was said to have paid a heavy fine for an attack on someone. A rick fire burnt most of his harvest and a hoard of gold sovereigns were stolen from him. On another occasion, a gun was fired into his bedroom when he was asleep there. A mirror was smashed and shot got embedded in the bed post but none of it caught Froude. The culprit of the crimes was never found.

He would go to any lengths to get his own back on people who thwarted him. Parson Jekyll, hearing hounds in his wood, went to investigate and found Froude's men digging out one of the breeding earths in March. He ordered them out. Froude was furious and threatened Jekyll, but the men went. Later police arrived with a search warrant; Froude had reported Jekyll for stealing his terrier. The premises were searched but of course no terrier was found.

On another occasion Froude made one of his curates drunk and then tied him up in a sack which he slung on a beam. The curate could not take the service and Froude refused to do so.

Bishop Phillpotts could not deal with him. Once when he tried to visit Froude his carriage sank in a pit filled with peat which Froude's men had dug in a stream bed. When Phillpotts wrote to Froude asking how many candidates he had for confirmation, the reply was that there were none because they had not yet reached the required standard and could not say the Lord's Prayer backwards. His note was scrawled on the back of a list of hounds that were ill with distemper!

If Baring-Gould's account of him is correct, Froude's marriage late in life seems to have been a shot-gun affair. He had been dallying with a Miss Hulse who was very much younger than he was. Her brothers were annoyed with his behaviour and when he visited them they got him so drunk that under pressure he signed a statement that he would marry the lady or pay £20 000. Some time later, when he was sober, he tried to treat the whole affair as a joke but he had to marry her.

The Revd John Arundel Radford, rector of Lapford, was nephew of John Froude and was of the same ilk. He too was used as a character in one of Blackmore's novels. Like his uncle he was a keen hunting man and when he took the service on Sunday his horse would be waiting for him in the vestry and his hounds in the churchyard.

He was a huge man and took part in wrestling at fairs. It is said that he used to hang up his surplice and invite anyone to tear it but no one dared. He once took on a whole gipsy encampment, wrestling with the men one by one, and won. He also frequented the navvy camps when the Exeter–Barnstaple railway was being built and challenged the men to wrestling matches.

He loved a fight and, according to Baring-Gould, was only once beaten, by a Welshman in Exeter. The next day he trailed the man to a remote cottage in Wales to give him a thrashing. He would even fight in a railway carriage and other travellers would bribe the guard to lock him in a carriage by himself. He gave his sons no money until they were able to knock him down. He had numerous illegitimate children in the village and was said to be responsible for the suicide of one of his servants after he had seduced her.

He was a drunkard and must have been an awesome figure when drunk and in a quarrelsome mood. He was often found drunk on Saturday nights in Exeter and taken to London Square, the assembly point for coaches and carts, where some form of transport would take him home.

He was frequently in debt and had writs issued against him. One rash tradesman, hoping to get his bill paid, took it to him. When there was no reply at the door, the man climbed through an open window. He found Radford cutting up the carcase of a pig with a very large knife. When the man proffered his bill, Radford cut two slices of bread, sandwiched the bill between them and made the poor man eat it while he threatened him with the knife.

His parishioners were naturally wary of such a violent man and, although he was an able preacher when he chose to preach, they forsook the church for the Nonconformist chapel. Pleas to the bishop were useless as he could not remove Radford who had inherited the advowson of the living from his family. Moreover, in his encounters with Bishop Phillpotts, Radford always seems to have been the victor, so the bishop was probably not keen to try to remove him.

The tale is told of Bishop Phillpotts trying to visit John Froude just as the latter was about to go hunting. Froude had to feign a highly infectious illness to get rid of the bishop quickly in order to be off with horse and hounds. The same story has been told of Radford.

Radford's atrocious behaviour had at last induced Phillpotts to suspend him and a curate took his place. When the curate did not turn up to take the Sunday service, someone went to look for him and found him in bed with his throat cut. It must have been terrifying for his successor when he was wakened by a man telling him to get out or he would suffer the same fate. Radford was taken to Exeter gaol, but although he was considered to be the culprit and known to have been in the area at the time, it could not be proved that he was guilty. It is reputed that he was acquitted because his parishioners said that they had never hanged a parson before and did not intend to start doing so.

He was reinstated but by then his congregation had deserted him and when he was old he used to weep when he took services attended only by his parish clerk, the clerk's son and one other man. When he died after thirty-five years as rector of Lapford, he left instructions for his burial in the chancel, with a threat to haunt the village if this was not done. But the parishioners refused to have him in the church and buried him in the churchyard by the vestry door.

Wrestling was very popular in some villages. In Countisbury church there was even a display of wrestling prizes – silver spoons and straw hat decked with ribbons. The vicar of Lanteglos-by-Fowey was a noted wrestler.

The Revd Robert Walsh, a leader in the Prayer-book Rebellion, was reputed to be a good wrestler as well as a good shot with the crossbow. Amongst the clergy archery was not necessarily for military purposes. It was often a feature of vicarage garden parties, indulged in even by the delicate ladies of the company in their long flounced dresses. The Revd C.J. Perry Keene, for forty-eight years vicar of Herrick's parish of Dean Prior, was an expert at the sport and was the Grand National Archery Champion for three years running. He seems to have been an all-round sportsman. He rode to hounds and won jumping contests and cups for hurdle-racing and rowing and at university was runner-up for the light-weight boxing championship.

J.H.B. Peel records that his great-great-grandfather, who was also a hunting parson, was a keen spectator at cock fights.

The Revd Jack Parsons of Liskeard was a noted cricketer who played for Warwickshire; he played in matches with such famous cricketers as W.G. Grace.

CHAPTER SEVEN

Shipwrecks and Smuggling

DEVON AND CORNWALL are notorious for the amount of smuggling and wrecking which went on there. Ships were lured on to rocks by some of the poverty-stricken people of these coasts to whom a wreck was a Godsend. However there seems to be no evidence of the parsons being wreckers or of their emulating Parson Troutbeck of the Scilly Isles who is reputed to have prayed not that ships would be wrecked but that if there were any wrecks that they should occur in the Scilly Isles for the benefit of the poor there. Parsons in other parts of the country are also credited with this prayer. Whilst not perhaps actively taking part in the wrecking, some of the parsons were not averse to collecting spoils from a wreck.

A story is told about the vicar of Breage, although it is also attributed to vicars of other parishes. He was preaching from the pulpit when there was news of a wreck. He shouted for the door of the church to be closed, quickly slipped out of his gown and pushed his way through the congregation to the door, saying, 'Now we'll all start fair.'

On the other hand priests have played their part in saving ships. In Britain lighthouses were often associated with the Church, sometimes with chantry chapels. The dissolution of the monasteries extinguished some of the fires which were the earliest form of warning light. Henry later granted a charter to the Guild of the Blessed Trinity, Newcastle, from which emerged the present Trinity House.

On Lantern Hill, overlooking the harbour of Ilfracombe, a small chapel was built and later altered so that in Henry VIII's reign it accommodated a 'lighthouse'. The warning fire was kept burning by members of the public who tended it as a penance to gain indulgences granted by the priest.

Church towers, such as that on the cliffs at Wembury, were often used by shipping to take their bearings. Carter, in *Cornish Shipwrecks*, says that the church tower of St Eval near Newquay was of such importance to shipping that when it collapsed in 1727 half of the money required to rebuild it was given by merchants and ship owners from Bristol. A huge cross at Dodman Point was built as a seamark. Its donor, the vicar of Caerhays, dedicated it and spent all night near it praying for those who were shipwrecked.

When ships came ashore, Hawker of Morwenstow had to protect any cargo from the wrecking instincts of the local people. The inhabitants of that part of the north Cornish coast had such a bad reputation as wreckers that when the *Juanita* was wrecked near Morwenstow at Duckpool, the coastguard who managed to board her after getting a rope aboard, found the captain standing with drawn sword in his cabin. Fortunately the coastguard managed to reassure him and the crew were saved.

Some parsons in Devon and Cornwall are said to have been actively associated with smuggling. The best known of these was the Revd Ambrose Stapleton who was vicar of East Budleigh for fifty-eight years. He must have been a popular vicar as he was a cheery sort of person who had his poor parishioners very much at heart. He also joined in their activities with zest, particularly smuggling in which most of the village was concerned. He let the smugglers meet at his home, 'Vicarsmead', and put the room above the porch at their disposal. The old vicarage (now a private house) was well equipped with secret hiding places for stowing contraband. According to tradition, Sir Walter Raleigh once went there as pupil to an earlier vicar.

Stapleton followed Matthew Mundy who was also a keen smuggler. They have both left their signatures on one of the window panes – 'Matt Mundy Vicr Sept 24 1741' and 'A.A. Stapleton Vicar 1794' – to celebrate their respective initiations into the smuggling fraternity. When the cargo was too large to be stored in the vicarage, extra storage space was found in the church and sometimes even the more capacious tombs in the churchyard were used. It is said that Stapleton used to haunt the roads in the guise of a ghost when a run was on to deter inquisitive onlookers. Unfortunately he drank too much of his own contraband.

Parson Dodge of Talland was said to be in league with smugglers and invented apparitions (which he was supposed to have eventually exorcized) to discourage excise men and others from frequenting the area during their runs.

One old smuggler said that he doubted whether there were any churches near the shore which had not had smuggled goods stored in them at some time and that the morning after a run there was always a good congregation in the church.

In Thurlestone church the goods were hidden above the porch behind the crenellations, the tower door being kept locked so that no one could look down on them. At Lelant the church was used on weekdays for storing contraband. In Duloe church the tubs of spirit were always stored on the side of the tower nearest the shore. In time that side was subjected to so much weight that the tower foundations sank and the tower had to be demolished and rebuilt. The parishioners had to pay for it but no doubt they had benefited by the casks stored there. The church spire of St Anthony-in-Roseland is supposed to have been used by smugglers to watch for the customs boat leaving Falmouth, though as David Mudd points out in *Around and about the Roseland* the customs men could have tricked the smugglers by approaching overland.

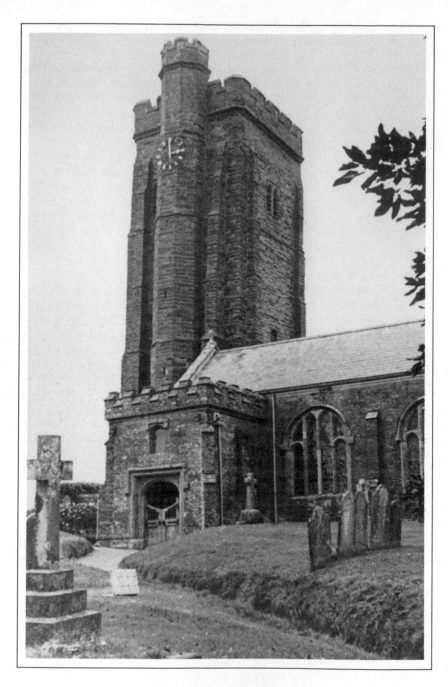

Thurlestone church

54

Some of the parsons might have been unaware that their churches were being used as repositories for smuggled goods, but the majority turned a blind eye and were rewarded by the occasional keg left on the doorstep, although they probably lectured their congregations on the evils of drink! Thurlestone parsons had enjoyed their share of the thriving smuggling trade until the Revd Peregrine Arthur Ilbert arrived and indignantly refused the perks. The former vicarage, now 'The Castle', at Stoke Gabriel has a tunnel running from the cellars which makes one wonder if the vicars there were in the smuggling business.

The Revd Richard Polwhele, when vicar of Manaccan, took over the wine in the cellar from the previous parson. He said that some of it was obviously smuggled wine as it tasted of salt water! According to Michael Williams in *Around Land's End*, it was a local parson who acted as assistant to the notorious Annie George, organizer of the smugglers and wreckers of Sennen.

Both the church and vicarage of Morwenstow had been used for smuggled goods before Parson Hawker's time. One of Hawker's servants, to whom he gave the fictitious name of Tristram Pentire, had been a smuggler and claimed that he was kidnapped by 'Cruel Coppinger', the infamous smuggler. It was no doubt from this servant that Hawker obtained his information for his writing on Coppinger. Pentire told Hawker of one occasion on which they bribed the sexton and put the goods under the church seats. The parson is said to have been amazed at the large congregation and to have preached a memorable sermon on 'Be not drunk with wine in excess'!

One Sunday there was a disturbance in the church porch, and people began to creep out of church. Finally the parson went to see what was going on. *The Black Prince*, Coppinger's boat, was being chased by a revenue cutter. Coppinger escaped by making for Gull Rock where it was too dangerous for the cutter to follow. The congregation cheered at the smuggler's escape and the parson then led them back to the church to finish the service.

Tristram Pentire told Hawker many stories of his smuggling exploits and methods which the parson put into his writings. One place known as 'the gauger's pocket' was a moss-covered hole in which the smuggler put a bribe of gold for the custom's man. Hawker himself drank very little.

Margaret A. Courtney in *Cornish Feasts and Folklore* quoted this letter from a Cubert parson to a well-known smuggler.

Martin Rowe, you very well know
That Cubert's vicar loves good liquor,
One bottles all, upon my soul,
You'll do right to come tonight;
My wife's banker, she'll pay for the anker.

CHAPTER EIGHT

Quarrels and Violence

PEOPLE TEND TO forget that parsons are human beings with the same failings as their fellow men. That this is so is apparent from a Launceston sexton's notebook which mentions a vicar in 1817 taking a burial service when tipsy. Another stole the Sunday offertories and got drunk on the wine for the sacrament. Then there were the parsons of Thelbridge and St Columb Minor, reported to Bishop Phillpotts for drinking more than was good for them. The Thelbridge parson appeared to be intoxicated in church sometimes and excused himself for not preaching a sermon by saying that he was unwell. A vicar of St Gerrans was accused of spending his nights as 'a carder and dicer'.

George Borlase, an eighteenth-century parson of South Petherwin was charged with bastardy but excused public penance on payment of £20. The Revd Thomas Wills of the parish of Wedron with Helston was said to have two illegitimate children. He was a keen huntsman and badger-baiter, but rarely preached in his churches. The rector of St Ives lost his living when he abducted and kept another man's wife. An eighteenth-century vicar of Colebrook did not escape so lightly for his immorality – he was excommunicated. Henry, rector of Hascumbe (Haccombe), according to the Hundred Rolls of Edward I stole land 'with appurtinances'. The vicar of St Merryn was deprived of his living in 1584 for receiving pirates' spoils.

The majority of the clergy, of course, led comparatively blameless lives. From 1739 to 1800 the Devon and Cornwall clergy were charged with only seven cases of immorality and two of these were dismissed. There were, however, the black sheep, like John Froude of Knowstone of whom it has been said that he was probably guilty of every sin in the calendar.

William Lang, vicar of Bradworthy, was charged with forty offences in the high court of parliament in 1641. Some of the charges were certainly exaggerated but he was still far from innocent.

He was a day labourer working on farms until he was thirty. Then he became the sheriff's bailiff and married in 1607. It was found that he had forged some warrants so he had to flee to Ireland. During his stay in Ireland he is said to have taken holy orders, but he had no university education and worked as a hireling reader until suspended by the Bishop of Exeter. He bought the living of Bradworthy by unlawful simony and made trouble amongst his parishioners by his numerous lucrative (to him) lawsuits and by running a kind of protection racket. He was also accused of poisoning his predecessor's wife, though that was probably not true as she lived sixteen years under his care. Other accusations included forgery, burning someone's barn and harvest, having a licence for the sale of wine, using the vicarage as a tavern, refusing to baptize a child or to do any duty on Sunday afternoon which he reserved for getting drunk at the alehouse, being rude to parishioners and other charges. His unfortunate parishioners must have been relieved when another vicar took his place in 1641. The gap in the list of vicars can still be seen as Lang neither died nor resigned in 1641 but was imprisoned.

Quarrels sometimes arose between the parson and his parishioners but these were often over trivial matters. Occasionally they reached a deadlock as in the case of Densham of Warleggan, referred to in Chapter 4.

A nineteenth-century rector of Stoke Dameral upset a family so much at a burial service by raising the fee for opening the family vault that they took the coffin home again and put it in a vault in their own garden. On another occasion there was friction over the burial of an army man who had died at a nearby hospital. The parson was occupied when the body was brought so an officer read the service and shots were fired over the grave. The vicar came rushing out when he heard the noise and was so furious that he had the body dug up again so that he could conduct a proper service.

According to medieval custom the best or next best possession of the deceased became the property of the Church. One rapacious Devon parson refused to bury a poor man unless he was given his only cow. Sir William Coffin, a great humanitarian, heard of this and threatened to bury the priest in the grave. When the priest still refused to carry out the burial he was seized, but capitulated before the threat was carried out. This case is said to have led to a much-needed investigation into burial fees. In 1396 there had been similar trouble in St Just-in-Roseland. Here the rector claimed a red surcoat. The relatives refused his demand and he retaliated by excommunicating them so they threatened to kill him. However, after shutting himself up in his rectory for safety for a time, during which no church services could be held, tempers seemed to have cooled.

Bishop Henry Phillpotts was noted for his litigation, sometimes against parsons of his own diocese. There were two particularly famous cases, one against the Revd James Shore of Berry Pomeroy and the other against the Revd Cornelius Goreham of St Just-in-Penwith. Phillpotts won the first case but eventually lost that against Goreham. The bishop believed that Goreham held views contrary to the doctrine of the Church and objected to his being offered the living of Brampford Speke.

Parson John Froude was also often involved in litigation. Once Cockburn (later Lord Chief Justice of England) as a young man won the

Bishop Phillpotts, from a painting dated 1851

case against Froude for his client. Afterwards Froude took Cockburn to lunch and said that he would always employ him for his law suits in future. Cockburn often stayed with him at Knowstone.

The rector of Calstock sued the abbot of Tavistock for tithe on the fish the abbot caught at the over-hatch. Unfortunately, several of his parishioners who supported his claim were convicted criminals and the rector lost his case.

Dr Cornelius Cardew had trouble with his parishioners at Lelant over payment of tithes and although a suite at the court of exchequer failed, he did eventually get the tithes. Tithes also seem to have caused trouble at St Ives, for in 1762, instead of giving the tenth cow and calf, some of the parishioners substituted butter and cheese and dumped it in the chancel during a service. The vicar refused to accept it and the parishioners refused to remove it, so there it stayed until it 'grew offensive' and the vicar had to ask the churchwarden to remove it. At Staverton church tithe animals were left in the chancel and eventually the parson had to put up a notice asking parishioners to leave them tied outside the porch.

A former Lynmouth parson's greed angered his parishioners. He imposed unreasonably large tithes on the boats that went out to catch the exceptional shoals of herrings sighted off the coast. The fishermen had no intention of paying his inflated tithes and put the story around that the large shoals had gone. The parson had to reduce his tithes to a reasonable level and then the shoals miraculously reappeared!

Some of the clerics could be violent despite their calling. Mention has already been made of the reputed murder of his curate by the Revd Radford. Sir John Laa or Large, a chaplain acting as curate at Staverton, was also accused of murder, according to Hemery, but was acquitted on the grounds of self-defence. One of his parishioners, named Gayne, had confronted him on Staverton Bridge, then a narrow wooden structure, and threatened him with a club. Gayne's wife had stood behind the cleric, preventing him escaping. Thus trapped, Sir John had attacked with a knife and mortally wounded Gayne.

Professor Hoskins mentioned the curious case of eleven incumbents who attacked the Dean of St Buryan and his assistants, badly injuring some of them. He also wrote of the rector of Combeinteignhead who, with two young men who were later to become bishop and archdeacon of Exeter, attacked the Dominican convent at Exeter which resulted in extensive damage to the brethren and their property, some of which the attackers stole.

The Revd Richard Bennet of St Neots and St Veep was accused of murdering his mistress. He had kept her in the vicarage, where she died. As she was buried at night in the church, her death was not detected until three years later. He was tried twice but, owing to lack of evidence, was acquitted. Later he was hanged for his support of the Prayer-book Rebellion.

In 1280, the vicar of Morwenstow took the law into his own hands and, at the head of a band of armed men, forced the vicar of Poundstock to surrender his living as he considered that his own living of Morwenstow was too poorly paid. The Archbishop of Canterbury went to Poundstock to reinstate the rightful vicar of the parish. The vicars of Poundstock seem to have been unfortunate: another, William de Penfound, was murdered on the chancel steps as he finished conducting mass and another Poundstock priest was hanged for his support of the Pilgrimage of Grace.

Some of the clergy were violent in their reception of John Wesley when he preached in the area. The Vicar of North Tawton and others brought a huntsman with hounds to deter Wesley from preaching. Symonds and Hoblyn, clergymen from St Ives, incited the crowd to harass Wesley. The

Revd Walter Borlase, a vicar of Madron and brother of the famous antiquarian, was particularly hostile to the Wesleys.

Ann Born mentions the ill-feeling which arose between the vicar of Modbury and the prior of a Benedictine community there. The prior, who shared the village church, annoyed the vicar as he had the larger share of the tithes. In retaliation, the vicar interred his late parishioners in extremely shallow graves directly under the prior's windows.

There was also a persistent feud between the Revd John Whitfield, an eighteenth-century parson of St Mary's church, Bideford, and the mayor and corporation of that town. According to Goodman, Whitfield not only took documents from the record room, but left the corpse of a child there for several months. He was summonsed and ordered to pay a heavy fine and costs, as well as having to return the stolen documents and repair the damage he had done in forcing an entrance.

Despite these incidents parsons were probably more often victims rather than aggressors. Francis Kilvert entered the following incident in his diary. At St Michael's church, Penkivel, a man in the congregation had an attack of insanity and, taking the parson's place at the desk, read the litany during the communion. The curate told him to stop but was told to 'get thee behind me Satan'. The rector then tried to stop him but the man hit him on the head with a very heavy prayer-book.

An eighteenth-century vicar of Tetcott was also the target for attack during his services. The eccentric squire, John Arscott, used to throw apples at him when he was not otherwise employed feeding church spiders on flies he had brought for them in a bottle. The guide to Mawnan church mentions a complaint by the rector in 1510 that the curate was going to mass in his best clothes when someone spit in his face and berated him.

In Exeter there was a strong feeling against the Whig-sponsored clergy after a man who had preached against the Whig government was brought to trial. This erupted into violence when it was believed that some of the clergy were hiding in the Ship Inn (once frequented by Drake, Hawkins, Grenville and Raleigh) and the mob tried to burn it down.

In her *A History of Chagford*, Jane Hayter-Hames records that in 1380 the Archdeacon of Totnes and his officers were attacked in Chagford churchyard. The culprits were excommunicated for their offences. Another attack on a parson occurred in Tavistock when the Abbot of Tavistock with some of his staff threw the poor parson out of his church and slashed his vestments with their swords, all because the abbot thought that he should have the collection.

Some parsons have met violent deaths in time of political unrest like Robert Walsh, of St Thomas church, Exeter, during the Prayer-book Rebellion. A few have been murdered: the Revd John Hay, vicar of South Brent in 1436, was dragged out of church, still in his vestments after vespers, and murdered in the churchyard.

In 1380 Walter Sancre of St Hilary was beheaded by a soldier. Three

Moreleigh church

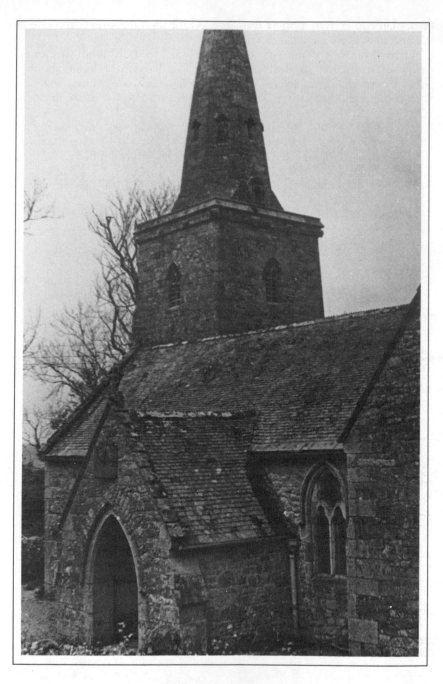

The church of St Hilary

years later in Penryn a priest was dragged through the streets and one at Cranstock was also assaulted.

Richard de Wydecombe of St Clement's church, Dartmouth was found drowned in 1329. It was said to be suicide, but there were doubts about it. Bishop Grandisson of Exeter did not think so and suspended services, bell-ringing and burial in the churchyard but relented to allow mass on Christmas Eve.

According to the church guide at Stoke Gabriel, an early owner of Waddeton furnished Waddeton chapel as a penance for killing the vicar during a heated argument. The parson of Woodleigh was killed in Edward I's reign by Sir Peter Fishacre during a violent quarrel over tithes. In expiation of his crime Sir Peter was ordered by the pope to build Moreleigh church, in the chancel of which he is buried.

In *Devon Mysteries* Judy Chard has written of another vicar's violent death. An unsatisfactory gardener asked the vicar of Teigngrace for a reference when he left. The rector wrote a derogatory statement about the man in Latin. When the gardener had been refused several jobs after showing the reference, he had it translated. He was so furious that he killed the vicar and stole his money and watch. After displaying the watch and boasting when drunk, he was caught and hanged in 1783.

Mob violence – though not from the parishioners – overwhelmed Bernard Walke. He has described it in his *Twenty Years at St Hilary*. He was from a family with a Catholic tradition which must have strongly influenced his own views.

After a curacy at Polruan, he and his artist wife, Annie, moved to St Hilary. Because of his Catholic leanings, some of his parishioners disapproved of his church services although he got on well with them personally.

He himself was a very peaceful character and it was not therefore surprising that he should be involved in the peace movement. One of their meetings ended in violence when it was broken up by the naval reserve who were holding a meeting nearby. Furniture was smashed and Walke was knocked unconscious.

Walke's own church was vandalized by two coachloads and two carloads of strangers. The only person he recognized amongst them was one who had obtained a Consistory Court judgement to take away some articles from the church. The raid was heartbreaking for Walke who took such pride in his church and had collected works of art for it. The vandals smashed a fifteenth-century font, damaged a memorial, destroyed a reredos by Ernest Proctor, removed statues and caused other damage. The parishioners cleared up the mess so that they could hold services again but these were interrupted by the troublemakers; the police had to be called and they summonsed some of them.

Walke had tuberculosis and spent eighteen months in a sanatorium, but he returned to St Hilary afterwards. In 1936 he retired to Mevagissey where he died.

The church of St Pancras, Widecombe-in-the-Moor

Bishop Edward Coppleston, who died in 1851 and was at one time rector of Offwell, was held up by a highwayman on a road leading into London. He was reputed to be the last person in Britain to be robbed by a highwayman.

John Prince, in his *Worthies of Devon*, described the violence experienced by the Revd George Lyde of Widecombe-in-the-Moor, caused not by men but by the elements. He was preaching in his church one Sunday in 1638 when it suddenly became so dark that the congregation could not see one another. Then the storm broke. The tower was struck, dislodging masonry which fell into the church. A lightning ball entered a window and went through the church burning those in its path including the parson's wife. Strangely, some people's underclothes were burnt but not their outer clothes. The parson wanted to stay in the church and pray but his congregation was naturally anxious to get out. Four of its members and a dog had been killed and many injured. A board bearing a long poem recording the catastrophe was erected in the church.

CHAPTER NINE

Memorials

A NUMBER OF churches in the two counties contain stained-glass-window memorials to clergymen, usually bought with subscriptions from their grateful parishioners. These windows are particularly interesting as not only do they depict religious scenes but often show episodes from the parson's life or local places associated with him and sometimes there is a portrait of the man himself.

Pillaton has stained-glass windows to former rectors. Godolphin has a window to a nineteenth-century priest who died as a result of visiting a smallpox victim. Holne, the birthplace of Charles Kingsley, has honoured him by putting a memorial window in the church. It includes a roundel portrait of him. Swimbridge church has a memorial window to Jack Russell.

Herrick's church of Dean Prior has three stained-glass windows to clergy: one behind the altar to Herrick, another to the Revd C. J. Perry Keene and one to the Revd R. C. Kitson. A particularly attractive feature of the Herrick window are the wild flowers which he mentions in his poems. It is unusual in that it has a portrait of Charles I, for Herrick was an ardent royalist. The words are from the carol he wrote.

'Passon Hawker' is commemorated in an interesting window in the church at Morwenstow. There are scenes from the life of John the Baptist and in addition little pictures connected with Hawker. He is there with his dog and so is St Morwenna so venerated by him. His beloved church and the figurehead of the *Caledonia* in the churchyard, the holy well of St John, the ownership of which he fought for and won, and other things that meant much to him are all depicted. The church also has memorial windows to two other vicars – to John Tarert and one given by him in memory of the Revd William Waddon Martyn.

Chudleigh has a window with an unusual story attached to it. The Revd Gilbert Burrington, who became vicar of Chudleigh in 1785, found a baby abandoned on his doorstep. He brought up the child and when John Williams, as he was called, grew up he became wealthy and was very generous to the people of Chudleigh. He never forgot his guardian's

St Mawes and the seal, commemorated in stained glass

kindness and when the vicar died, to show his gratitude he commissioned the stained-glass window in his memory. It was installed in 1847; in 1981 an appeal was launched to raise money to repair it.

The church of St Mawes has three clear-glass windows each with an attractive scene in stained glass depicting events from the life of St Mawes. In one he is accompanied by a very appealing seal. This refers to the story of St Mawes teaching his pupils as he sat on his rock chair on the shore, when a seal joined them; it would not stop barking until St Mawes slapped its head, when it hastily left his class. The windows are in memory of Francis Harcourt Barnaby, an assistant priest there.

A few churches have bells as memorials to their parsons. In Cadeleigh there is a treble bell to the memory of the Revd Paul Ford Britton who died in 1902 after being rector of the parish for fifty-seven years. At Morwenstow lines from Hawker's poem, The Silent Tower of Bottreaux,

> Come to thy God in time
> Come to thy God at last

are inscribed on the leading bell which is dedicated to him. One of the bells in Kilkhampton church is in memory of the Revd Roderick Dew. The Thomas Tanners, father and son, who between them ministered for ninety years, have the sixth bell of the peal to their memory.

In Stokeinteignhead there is a very early brass of a priest in mass vestments – alb, chasuble, manaple and stole. The identity of the priest is not known but may possibly be John Symon, a rector of the parish and canon of Exeter who died in 1497. The little figure is now let into mosaic at the side of the altar, but at one time, having become separated from its stone, it was nailed on to the back of the door. It is popular with brass-rubbers, so a copy has been made from which rubbings can be taken and the original is protected from further use. This ancient brass is a palimpsest, on the reverse is an engraving of another priest made in 1496.

Another interesting palimpsest is an engraving of a priest at Yealmpton. It is a fifteenth-century piece of brass of the head of a priest with the figure of God holding a shroud round his soul. This engraving was Flemish. The side of the brass now uppermost and under a canopy is to Isobel Copleston and was engraved in 1580. Curiously, another part of the original brass has been found under the altar at Denham, near Eye in Suffolk.

Cornwall's most ancient brass is of a priest, Thomas Awmarle, in Cardinham church. He was rector of the church from 1356 until his death in 1400. He is depicted with a tonsure, wearing a buttoned cassock and, incongruously, a sword. Two shields below the brass indicate aristocratic lineage. Blisland's rector, John Balsam, is commemorated by another very early brass dating from 1410 and Padstow has a brass memorial of 1421 to Laurence Merther, a vicar of the parish.

Early priests were often buried with a chalice. It is not unusual to find a chalice engraved on priests' brasses or on the coffin lid which formed part

The inscription on the bust reads:

ZACHARY MUDGE
PREBENDARY OF EXETER
AND VICAR OF
ST. ANDREW'S, PLYMOUTH
BORN 1694 · DIED 1769
IN PRIVATE LIFE HE WAS
AMIABLE AND BENEVOLENT
IN HIS MINISTRY FAITHFUL
ELOQUENT AND PERSUASIVE
DISTINGUISHED
FOR KNOWLEDGE AMONG THE
LEARNED AND FOR TALENT
AMONG MEN OF SCIENCE

Chantrey's bust of the Revd Zachary Mudge in St Andrew's church

of the pavement in some churches. The chalice was accompanied by a cross and paten, insignia of priestly status.

There are sixteenth-century brasses to priests at Penkivel and Wendron. In the church of St Just-in-Roseland there is a brass of about 1520 of a priest in a choir cope.

Tedburn St Mary has a brass dating from 1663 of a rector, his wife, son and three daughters. The rector wears a gown and hood. Another brass showing a priest surrounded by his family is in Harford church, though the memorial is not to the priest but to one of the sons. All the family – father, mother and nine of the children – are dressed in black and kneel on a black and white tiled floor, but the priestly son, John Prideaux, is in the red robes of a doctor of divinity. He was chaplain to James I, became Bishop of Worcester, but died in poverty after being removed from office in the Civil War. One of the sixteen children of Roger Kyngdon is also dressed as a priest in a brass of 1471 in Quethiock church.

In St Saviour's church, Dartmouth, there is a replica of a brass. It commemorates John Flavel who was an intruding parson in the Commonwealth. He was turned out at the Restoration and became a Dissenting minister. He was buried at St Saviour's but some years later bigoted members of the congregation demanded the removal of his memorial brass. His followers moved it to the meeting-house and later to Flavel church. The replica was placed in St Saviour's in 1885.

There is an ancient altar tomb of a priest in Morthoe church, the carving of its occupant holding a chalice is now almost worn away. He was Sir William de Tracy, a rector in the church in the fourteenth century. It is said that robbers stole the lead enclosing the body and as a consequence never prospered afterwards. His kinsman, another Sir William de Tracy, was one of Thomas Becket's murderers.

Few could have had more illustrious men to commemorate them than Zachary Mudge, for his bust in St Andrew's church in Plymouth was carved by the famous sculptor Sir Francis Chantrey from a single block of marble. It was based on a painting by Sir Joshua Reynolds and the epitaph was written by Dr Johnson. The monument was damaged in the blitz but the head was recovered from the debris and is still in the church.

The martyr's pulpit in Exeter Cathedral is in memory of Bishop Patterson who was killed by the inhabitants of Melanesia.

At Hartland a carved litany desk and wall panelling and carving commemorate two of the clergy who served there. There is a strange memorial to the Revd John Fortescue in Poltimore church; it is a carved bench-end depicting him and his wife, but only the wife is given a halo.

There is a particularly beautiful memorial to the Revd E. Pinwill who was rector at Ermington for nearly fifty years. It is the fine wood-carving done by his daughter, Violet Pinwill. In the sanctuary is a carved panel showing the church and in the lady chapel are commemorative altar rails. The church contains much of her work, including a reredos, pulpit, carved bench-ends, font cover and screens.

Wood carving by Violet Pinwill in Ermington church

The Revd George Polgrean of St Blazey will not readily be forgotten as the church clock is a memorial to him and a street there is named after him. A constant reminder of the Revd H. F. Lyte is the carillon in All Saints church, Brixham, which plays his hymns 'Abide with me', 'Praise, my soul, the King of Heaven' and 'Pleasant are thy courts above' at certain times of the day. Nor will the Revd James Hannington, who became Bishop of East Equatorial Africa, be easily forgotten in Martinhoe as the village hall was built in memory of him.

Bibliography

Appleyard, J. *Henry Francis Lyte M.A. (Author of 'Abide with me'): A Short Biography* (Epworth Press, 1939)

Baker, F. *The Call of Cornwall* (Hale, 1976)

Baring-Gould, S. *A Book of Dartmoor* (Wildwood House, new edition 1982)

Baring-Gould, S. *Devonshire Characters and Strange Events* (Bodley Head, 1908)

Baring-Gould, S. *Early Reminiscences 1834–1864* (Bodley Head, 1923)

Baring-Gould, S. *Further Reminiscences* (Bodley Head, 1925)

Baring-Gould, S. *Old Country Life* (EP Publishing, new edition 1975)

Baring-Gould, S. *The Vicar of Morwenstow* (Methuen, 1899)

Bax, B.A. *The English Parsonage* (John Murray, 1964)

Bell, A. *Sydney Smith. A Biography* (Clarendon Press, 1980)

Borlase, W. *Antiquities Historical and Monumental of the County of Cornwall,* second edition with a new introduction by P.A.S. Pool and C. Thomas (EP Publishing in collaboration with Cornwall County Library, 1973)

Born, A. *South Devon. Combe Tor and Seascape* (Gollancz, 1983)

Botrell, W. *Traditions and Hearthside Stories of West Cornwall* (Penzance, 1870)

Brendon, P. *Hawker of Morwenstow: Portrait of a Victorian Eccentric* (Cape, 1975)

Brown, H.M. *What to Look For in Cornish Churches* (David & Charles, 1973)

Byles, C.E. *The Life and Letters of R.S. Hawker (sometime Vicar of Morwenstow)* (Bodley Head, 1906)

Chard, J. *Devon Mysteries* (Bossiney Books, 1979)

Chitty, S. *The Beast and the Monk. A Life of Charles Kingsley* (Hodder & Stoughton, 1974)

Chitty, S. *Charles Kingsley's Landscape* (David & Charles, 1976)

Colloms, B. *Charles Kingsley, the Lion of Eversley* (Constable, 1975)

Courtney, M.A. *Cornish Feasts and Folklore* (EP Publications, 1973, reprinted from the 1890 edition)

Creswell, B.F. *A Book of Devonshire Parsons* (Heath Cranton, 1932)

Davies, E.W.L. (Otter) *A Memoir of the Reverend John Russell and his Out-of-door Life* (Richard Bentley, 1883)

Davies, G.C.B. *Henry Phillpotts, Bishop of Exeter 1778–1869* (S.P.C.K., 1954)

Dickinson, B.H.C. *Sabine Baring-Gould, Squarson, Writer and Folklorist 1834–1924* (David & Charles, 1970)

Foot, S. *Hawker of Morwenstow* (Bossiney Books, 1980)

Garland, H.J. *Henry Francis Lyte and the Story of 'Abide with me'* (Torch Publishing, 1956)

Goodenough, S. *The Country Parson* (David & Charles, 1983)

Graham, F. *Smuggling in Devon* (Published by the author, 1965)

Hawker, R.S. *Footprints of Former Men in Far Cornwall* (John Russell Smith, 1903)

Hayter-Haymes, J. *A History of Chagford* (Phillimore, 1981)

Hemery, E. *Historic Dart* (David & Charles, 1982)

Hinde, T. *A Field Guide to the English Country Parson* (Heinemann, 1984)

Hoskins, W.G. *Devon* (David & Charles, 1972)

Hunt, P.J. *Devon's Age of Elegance* (Devon Books, 1984)

Keene, C.J.P. *Herrick's Parish, Dean Prior, with Stories and Songs of Dean Bourn* (Wm Brendon, Plymouth)

Kingsley, F. *Charles Kingsley. His Letters and Memories of His Life* Edited by his wife (Scribner, Armstrong & Co., 1877)

Lee, F.G. *Memorials of the late Rev Robert Stephen Hawker M.A., sometime vicar of Morwenstow in the diocese of Exeter* (Chatto & Windus, 1876)

Martin, L. C. *The Poetical Works of Robert Herrick* (Oxford University Press, 1956)

Martin, W.K. *Over the Hills* (Michael Joseph, 1968)

Maurier, D. Du *Vanishing Cornwall* (Penguin, 1978)

Mee, A. *The King's England: Cornwall* (Hodder & Stoughton, 1967)

Mee, A. *The King's England: Devon* (Hodder & Stoughton, 1965)

Moorman, F.W. *Robert Herrick. A Biographical and Critical Study* (Lane, 1910)

Mudd, D. *Around and about the Roseland* (Bossiney Books, 1980)

Purcell, W.E. *'Onward Christian Soldier', a Life of Sabine Baring-Gould, Parson, Squire, Novelist, Antiquary, 1834–1924* (Longman, 1957)

Rendell, J. *Hawker Country* (Bossiney Books, 1980)

Slader, J.M. *The Churches of Devon* (David & Charles, 1968)

Skinner, B.G. *Henry Francis Lyte, Brixham's Poet and Priest* (University of Exeter, 1974)

Thornton, W.H. *Reminiscences and Reflections of an Old West-country Clergyman* (Iredale, 1897–9)

Turner, J. *Ghosts of the south west* (David & Charles, 1973)

Walke, B. *Twenty Years at St Hilary* (Methuen, 1936)

Warne, A. *Church and Society in Eighteenth-century Devon* (David & Charles, 1969)

Wood, G.B. *Smugglers' Britain* (Cassell, 1966)

In addition many of the interesting guides in the various churches visited have supplied useful material.